D1389893

Acclaim for Stephen Breyer's

ACTIVE LIBERTY

"Fluid.... Should show up on every litigator's bookshelf, providing how-to advice like a do-it-yourself guidebook to judicial reasoning."
—*New York Law Journal*

"Breyer's prose is admirably simple and clear, and his discussion shows a keen legal intellect that espouses broad values rather than narrow theories, and a deep, humane concern with fostering democracy and the well-being of the citizenry. This will be essential reading at a possibly watershed moment for the Supreme Court."
—*Publishers Weekly* (starred review)

"Impeccable advice for the powerful in all walks of life.... Breyer has earned a reputation as one of the Supreme Court's more coherent thinkers."
—*The Boston Globe*

"Rather than looking exclusively to the past, Breyer appreciates the need to engage the Constitution as a living document." —*Booklist*

"A good introduction to how judges observe the rule of law. Written in clear language for the lay reader—though backed by scholarly notes." —*Library Journal*

"A breath of fresh air.... His calm tone, straightforward language, wise understanding of the judicial craft, and respectful engagement with rival views could not be more timely." —*Policy Review*

STEPHEN BREYER

ACTIVE LIBERTY

Stephen Breyer is a Justice of the Supreme Court of the United States. He is a resident of Cambridge, Massachusetts, and Washington, D.C.

ALSO BY STEPHEN BREYER

Administrative Law and Regulatory Policy
(coauthor Richard Stewart)

Breaking the Vicious Circle

Regulation and Its Reform

ACTIVE LIBERTY

ACTIVE LIBERTY

Interpreting A
Democratic Constitution

STEPHEN BREYER

OXFORD
UNIVERSITY PRESS

OXFORD
UNIVERSITY PRESS

Great Clarendon Street, Oxford OX2 6DP

Oxford University Press is a department of the University of Oxford.
It furthers the University's objective of excellence in research, scholarship,
and education by publishing worldwide in

Oxford New York

Auckland Cape Town Dar es Salaam Hong Kong Karachi
Kuala Lumpur Madrid Melbourne Mexico City Nairobi
New Delhi Shanghai Taipei Toronto

With offices in

Argentina Austria Brazil Chile Czech Republic France Greece
Guatemala Hungary Italy Japan Poland Portugal Singapore
South Korea Switzerland Thailand Turkey Ukraine Vietnam

Oxford is a registered trade mark of Oxford University Press
in the UK and in certain other countries

Published in the United States
by Oxford University Press Inc., New York

British Library Cataloguing in Publication Data

Data available

Library of Congress Cataloging in Publication Data
Breyer, Stephen G., 1938-
Active liberty: interpreting a democratic Constitution / Stephen
Breyer.–New ed.
   p. cm
Includes bibliographical references and index.
ISBN-13: 978-0-19-922707-5 (acid-free paper)   1. Constitutional
law—United States—Interpretation and construction.   2. Law–United
States–Interpertation and construction.   3. Judicial process—United
States.   4. Constituent power–United States.   5. Liberty.   I. Title.
KF4552.B74 2008
342.73—dc22   2007050468

Typeset by Newgen Imaging Systems (P) Ltd., Chennai, India
Printed in Great Britain
on acid-free paper by
Biddles Ltd., King's Lynn

ISBN 978-0-19-922707-5

1 3 5 7 9 10 8 6 4 2

To my brother and fellow judge,
Chuck

Contents

Acknowledgments

This book originally took the form of the Tanner Lectures on Human Values presented at Harvard University in 2004. Gordon Wood and Robert George provided valuable commentary on those lectures. The University of Utah Press will publish an archival copy of the lectures and commentary. I presented an initial version of the Tanner Lectures as the James Madison Lecture at New York University Law School in 2001 (published as *Our Democratic Constitution*, 77 New York University Law Review, 2002).

I am grateful indeed for the time, effort, and advice of Paul Gewirtz and Robert Henry. I also very much appreciate the constructive commentary of the people who have read earlier drafts of this work, including Akhil Amar, Michael Boudin, Erwin Chemerinsky, Norman Dorsen, Ronald Dworkin, William Eskridge, Owen Fiss, Charles Fried, Elizabeth Garrett, Richard Pildes, Richard Posner, Robert Post, and Laurence Tribe; and, a special thanks, too, to Emma Rothschild. Their critiques, their ideas, and their suggestions have helped me enormously, adding much of value to the enterprise. I thank Antoine

Garapon for his help in creating a British and European edition. I thank Patricia Hass, my editor, and the others at Knopf who worked long, hard, and effectively at bringing this book to publication. I thank John Louth for his help with this British edition. I thank these and others as well for their many contributions.

ACTIVE LIBERTY

INTRODUCTION

This book focuses upon the American constitutional system and, in particular, upon the role of the United States Supreme Court in interpreting the Constitution. (Indeed, when I say "Constitution" I normally mean the American Constitution). The American Constitution, unlike that of Britain, is a written constitution. The American Congress, unlike Britain's Parliament, is not legislatively supreme but is directly bound by the Constitution's provisions. These and other differences mean that a British or European reader may find it difficult to understand some of the constitutional and institutional assumptions I make in this book. To facilitate that reader's task, I shall mention several basic characteristics of the Constitution and the Supreme Court that will help readers outside America place the subsequent discussion in proper context.

First, the United States Constitution, adopted in 1789, is a succinct written document of fewer than 10,000 words set forth in seven articles and twenty-seven subsequent amendments. The Constitution establishes the institutions of the federal government and imposes limitations upon the exercise of governmental power. The Constitution's articles divide power among three co-equal branches of federal government: a Legislative Branch with two houses, the Senate and the House of Representatives; an Executive Branch headed by the President; and a Judicial Branch consisting of a Supreme Court and lower federal courts. The Constitution's original ten amendments (the "Bill of Rights") and the three amendments adopted in the aftermath of the American Civil War protect important individual liberties from invasion by federal and state governments.

The federal Constitution also foresees the continued existence of strong States. There are now fifty States. And each has its own state constitution, typically providing for a state legislature, a state governor, and a state judicial system.

Second, American constitutional law reflects the deeply embedded American view that "the people" constitute the ultimate, and only legitimate, source of law. Thus, James Madison, the Constitution's chief author, wrote that the Constitution is a "charter...of power...granted by liberty," not (as in Europe) a "charter of liberty granted by power." And the Constitution's Tenth Amendment states that the "powers not delegated" to the federal government "by the Constitution, nor prohibited by it to the States are reserved to the States respectively or to the people." Unless one can trace a clear (and not too distant) line of legal authority between an individual law or legal institution and "the people," the law or institution seems illegitimate. When, for example, contemporary

Introduction

Americans ask about international tribunals, "But who are the judges on these tribunals? Who appoints them?" they are looking for a clear and not too distant line of authority—from the judge to the American people.

Third, the Constitution creates in the Judicial Branch of the federal government a Supreme Court of the United States. That Court currently consists of nine judges, eight men and one woman. The Constitution says that the President of the United States shall nominate "Judges of the supreme Court" and that the Senate, by majority vote, must confirm the nominee. It adds that the judges "shall hold their Offices during good Behaviour"; that language has been taken to mean that judges of the Supreme Court (who are called "Justices") possess life tenure.

The Constitution does not specify any particular professional qualification for appointment. The 110 judges who have served on the Court have come from different professional backgrounds. In the past, Presidents have appointed Senators, Governors, and even a former President of the United States. But all nine current members come from professional backgrounds that include prior judicial service—in each instance as a judge of a federal court of appeals. Prior to their judicial appointments, four had been professors of law and five had been active in practice, either with the government or with private law firms.

Fourth, the Supreme Court's jurisdiction covers questions involving the Constitution of the United States, federal statutes, and other forms of federal law (e.g., federal administrative rules). It does *not* decide matters of state law. This limitation is important; for most American law is state law, not federal law. Virtually all family law, and most property, accident, testamentary, criminal, and business law is state law. Even education law and environmental law is largely state law. And state supreme courts, not the United States Supreme Court, have the final word as to the interpretation of state law.

Federal statutory and agency law is, of course, highly important, ranging in subject matter from interstate commerce and civil rights to health, welfare, social security and environmental protection (and much else besides). But one should keep in mind that federal law comprises only a fraction of the American legal universe.

Fifth, the Supreme Court normally has the final word as to the validity of any law challenged as contrary to the provisions of the federal Constitution. The federal Constitution trumps lower forms of law, for example, statutory law, whether state or federal. Early on in American history, the Supreme Court assumed the power to strike down a *state* law that conflicts with federal statutory law or with the federal Constitution. And in the famous case of *Marbury v Madison* the Court assumed the power to strike down a *federal* law that conflicts with the federal Constitution.

To overcome a Court holding that a law is unconstitutional, the public must amend the Constitution.

Introduction

And that is not easy to accomplish. An amendment first requires the agreement of two-thirds of each house of Congress (or the calling of a special constitutional convention—which has never been done) followed by ratification by the legislatures of three-quarters of the States. Since the Bill of Rights became part of the Constitution more than 200 years ago, only seventeen amendments have been enacted. And only four directly overturned Supreme Court decisions. Thus, the Supreme Court's determination that a law is unconstitutional is normally authoritative and final.

Sixth, the Court itself possesses the discretionary authority to choose among the many requests that it hear particular cases. And the Court exercises its discretionary authority with care. A few quantitative estimates will help the reader understand how the Supreme Court creates the docket of cases that it will decide.

The federal issues that the Court considers may arise in either state courts or federal courts (though federal questions are somewhat more likely to be present in federal court cases). The state court systems, taken together, handle several million cases each year. The smaller federal court system handles about 250,000 cases. Many of these cases settle out of court, and many of the remaining controversies are resolved in the course of trial and appeal. After this winnowing, the number of cases that still contain a federal issue falls to about 100,000. In about 8,000 of these cases, a losing party will seek review in the

Supreme Court. The Court typically grants 80 to 100 such requests annually.

The numbers make clear that the Supreme Court could not possibly consider all plausible claims that a lower court decision is legally erroneous. Nor does it try to do so. Rather, the Court's basic task is to provide a nationally uniform interpretation of the Constitution or other federal law where it sees a need for consistency. It typically finds such a need where lower courts have come to different conclusions about the meaning of the same provision of the Constitution or a federal statute. The upshot is that each year the Supreme Court will consider only a small number of legal questions, all of which involve federal issues, many of which are statutory in nature, and only a handful of which require the Court to interpret the Constitution of the United States.

CHAPTER ONE

ACTIVE LIBERTY

The United States is a nation built upon principles of liberty. That liberty means not only freedom from government coercion but also the freedom to participate in the government itself. When Jefferson wrote, "I know no safe depository of the ultimate powers of the society but the people themselves," his concern was for abuse of government power. But when he spoke of the rights of the citizen as "a participator in the government of affairs," when Adams, his rival, added that all citizens have a "positive passion for the public good," and when the Founders referred to "public liberty," they had in mind more than freedom from a despotic government. They had invoked an idea of freedom as old as antiquity, the freedom of the individual citizen to participate in the government and thereby to share with others the right to make or to control the nation's public acts.[1]

Writing thirty years after the adoption of the American Constitution and the beginnings of the French Revolution, the political philosopher Benjamin Constant emphasized the differences between these two kinds of liberty. He called them "the liberty of the ancients" and the "liberty of the moderns." He described "the liberty of the ancients" as an active liberty. It consisted of a sharing of a nation's sovereign authority among that nation's citizens. From the citizen's perspective it meant "an active and constant participation in collective power"; it included the citizen's right to "deliberate in the public place," to "vote for war or peace," to "make treaties," to "enact laws," to examine the actions and accounts of those who administer government, and to hold them responsible for their misdeeds. From the nation's perspective, it meant "submitting to all the citizens, without exception, the care and assessment of their most sacred interests." This sharing of sovereign authority, Constant said, "enlarged" the citizens' "minds, ennobled their thoughts," and "established among them a kind of intellectual equality which forms the glory and the power of a people." [2]

At the same time, ancient liberty was incomplete. It failed to protect the individual citizen from the tyranny of the majority. It provided a dismal pretext for those who advocated new "kinds of tyranny." Having seen the Terror, Constant was well aware of the dangers of subjecting the individual to the unconstrained "authority of the group"; and he warned against "borrowing from the ancient republics the means" for governments "to oppress us." Constant argued that governments must protect the "true modern liberty." That liberty, "civil liberty," freedom from government, consisted of the individual's freedom to pursue his own interests and desires free of improper government interference.[3]

Constant argued that both kinds of liberty—ancient and modern—are critically important. A society that overemphasizes ancient liberty places too low a value upon the individual's right to freedom from the majority. A society that overemphasizes modern liberty runs the risk that citizens, "enjoying their private independence and in the pursuit of their individual interests," will "too easily renounce their rights to share political power." We must "learn to combine the two together."[4]

In this book, while conscious of the importance of modern liberty, I seek to call increased attention to the combination's other half. I focus primarily upon the active liberty of the ancients, what Constant called the people's right to "an active and constant participation in collective power." My thesis is that courts should take greater account of the Constitution's democratic nature when they interpret constitutional and statutory texts. That thesis encompasses well-known arguments for judicial modesty: The judge, compared to the legislator, lacks relevant expertise. The "people" must develop "the political experience" and they must obtain "the moral education and stimulus that come from . . . correcting their own errors." Judges, too, must display that doubt, caution, and prudence, that not being "too sure" of oneself, that one of America's greatest judges, Judge Learned Hand, described as "the spirit of liberty."[5]

But my thesis reaches beyond these classic arguments. It finds in the Constitution's democratic objective not simply restraint on judicial power or an ancient counterpart of more modern protection, but also a source of judicial authority and an interpretive aid to more effective protection of ancient and modern liberty alike. It finds a basic perspective that helps make sense of our Constitution's structure, illuminating aspects that otherwise seem less coherent. Through examples, my thesis illustrates how emphasizing this democratic objective can bring us closer to achieving the proper balance to which Constant referred. The examples suggest that increased emphasis upon that objective by judges when they interpret a legal text will yield better law—law that helps a community of individuals democratically find practical solutions to important contemporary social problems. They simultaneously illustrate the importance of a judge's considering practical consequences, that is, consequences valued in terms of constitutional purposes, when the interpretation of constitutional language is at issue.

Active liberty and the history of the American Constitution

Is it reasonable from a historical perspective to view the Constitution as centrally focused upon active liberty, upon the right of individuals to participate in democratic self-government? I believe so. I have already listed various constitutional provisions that specifically further that objective. And the now standard historical accounts of the writing of the Constitution—in the works, for example, of Gordon Wood and Bernard Bailyn—make clear that active liberty, the principle of participatory self-government, was a primary force shaping the system of government that the document creates.[6]

The primarily democratic nature of the Constitution's governmental structure has not always seemed obvious. John Adams, one of the Constitution's authors and America's second President, understood the Constitution as seeking to create an Aristotelian "mixed" form of government. Our government, like the British government, would reflect the structure of eighteenth-century society. The House of Representatives, like the House of Commons, would constitute the "democratical branch" of the new federal government, embodying the people's basic decency and common sense. The Senate, like the House of Lords, would represent the aristocratic element of society, embodying its wisdom while checking the people's sometimes "barbarous...and cruel" passions. The Executive would represent the monarchical element of society, with the President serving as a mediator, a balancer, helping to keep social forces in equilibrium.[7]

But Adams himself recognized that his notions of constitutionalism were not widely shared. And historians now tell us that by the time the Constitution was ratified by the states, the more "aristocratic" concept held by some of the Framers was a minority view. Rather, the document created a governmental structure that reflected the view that sovereign authority originated in the people; that the "Right to legislate is originally in every Member of the Community." An important imperative modified but also reinforced this right, namely the need to protect individual liberty (i.e., the liberty of the moderns). The right was also subject to an important constraint, namely the need for workable government. The term "every Member" did not then include women or slaves; the "Community" was not theirs. But the Constitution's structure, viewed in terms of the narrow "Community" of the time, was nonetheless democratic and set the stage for that community's later democratic expansion.[8]

Democracy, of course, could not mean a Greek city-state. The nation's geographic size, along with its large and growing population, would prevent replication at the national level of the Athenian agora or a New England town meeting. The people would have to delegate the day-to-day work of governance. But the people could continue to share sovereign authority; they could continue to participate actively in the governing processes. "Delegated democracy" need not represent a significant departure from democratic principle.[9]

Moreover, in the view of modern historians, much post-revolutionary (pre-constitutional) American political thought was characterized by suspicion of government, hostility to the Executive Branch, and confidence in democracy as the best check upon government's oppressive tendencies. The former colonists, now Americans, saw "radical destruction" of "magisterial authority" as the way—perhaps the only way—to keep power in check, to prevent its arbitrary exercise. They embraced the concept of "public liberty," believing that "liberty in a State is self-government." They considered a free people to be a people that government cannot oppress, for the reason that the people have "a constitutional check upon the power to oppress." Thus, during the time between the end of the Revolutionary War and the writing of the Constitution, the American public came to the conclusion that democratic principles must underlie the structure of post-revolutionary government.[10]

After the Revolution the citizens of many former colonies translated their democratic beliefs into highly democratic forms of state government. Pennsylvania, for example, experimented with a constitution that abolished the position of governor, substituting a twelve-member elected council; created a unicameral legislature with one-year terms; imposed strict four-year term limits; insisted that all public decision-making take place in public; and provided for a board of censors, a kind of statewide grand jury with separately elected members who would investigate all actions by the legislature and report to the public. Indeed, in many of the colonies governors were forbidden to participate in the lawmaking function; impeachment was common; and terms of office were short. Most Americans accepted the Whig maxim, "where annual elections end, tyranny begins."[11]

Why then did the Framers not write and the states not ratify a Constitution that contained similar democratic structures? Why did they not, like Pennsylvania, approximate a closer-to-Athenian version of democracy? Why did they create so complex a form of government, placing more distance between electors and elected than even the needs of "delegation" of democratic authority might demand?

The reason, in part, is that experience with many of these initial forms of democratic government had proved disappointing. Pennsylvanians found that their government enacted conflicting policies, reflecting the vagaries of shifting public opinion; that through debt repudiation it had produced an insecure climate for business; and that those within government—a continuously changing group—were often at war with one another. Similarly, Massachusetts saw in Shays's Rebellion a public that would fight to avoid not only debt repayment but also taxation of any sort. Other states had faced similar, though perhaps less dramatic, difficulties.[12]

Nonetheless, despite these difficulties, the Framers did not abandon their basically democratic outlook. That is the main point. They wrote a Constitution that begins with the words "We the People." The words are not "we the people of 1787." Rather their words, legal scholar Alexander Meiklejohn tells us, mean that "it is agreed, and with every passing moment it is re-agreed, that the people of the United States shall be self-governed."[13]

The Constitution subsequently implements its preamble by vesting legislative power in a House of Representatives and a Senate—both bodies made up of individuals who are ultimately responsible to the people. Article I specifies that members of the House will be "chosen every second Year by the People of the several States," i.e., by voters who "shall have the qualifications requisite for electors of the most numerous branch of the state legislature." That article also originally specified that senators would be "chosen by" state "legislatures." But in so specifying, the Framers did not seek to model the "Senate" upon the House of Lords. Rather, eighteenth-century supporters of a Senate argued that this second legislative body would *increase* democracy by providing for "double representation." They pointed out that citizens chose their state legislators through elections. And given the importance of the senatorial position, it seems likely that the voters would have held their state legislators to account for their national senatorial choices.[14]

Article II vests executive power in a President, selected by an Electoral College, not the voters. But this mechanism does not create a presidency free from democratic control. Rather, the Constitution grants state legislators, elected by, and accountable to, the people, the power to determine how to select the state's electors. In 1789, this meant election by legislators in five states, by the people in four states, and by mixed methods in two states (two states did not participate). By 1832 it meant electors chosen directly by the people in every state but South Carolina (which switched to popular election after the Civil War). This popular connection now means (and meant at the time) that the President and senators would consider themselves responsible to, or representing the interests of, not a particular social class, but "We the People." [15]

Thus, James Wilson, an influential figure at the Constitutional Convention, summed up the Framers' conception of the nonlegislative branches as follows:

> The executive, and judicial power are now drawn from the same source, are now animated by the same principles, and are now directed to the same ends, with the legislative authority: they who execute, and they who administer the laws, are so much the servants, and therefore as much the friends of the people, as those who make them. [16]

And John Taylor, writing in 1790, described the Constitution's structure in terms that are difficult to reconcile with a retreat from democratic principle. "Power," he said, "is first divided between the government and the people, reserving to the people, the control of the dividend allotted to the government." The government's allotment of power is then "distributed in quotas still more minute" to its various branches. But though the power is dispersed, the people themselves continue to control the policy-making activities of these different branches of government. [17]

One might argue that these descriptions vastly over-state the Framers' commitment to democracy. As I have just said, the Constitution seems to create a governmental structure far more complex, and in part far more distant from the people, than principles of delegated democracy demand. Does not that fact reflect a profound retreat from democratic structure, in the direction, as Adams suggested, of aristocratic government?

Not necessarily so. That is because we can find in these same constitutional facts not so much a retreat from democratic principle as an effort to produce a government committed to democratic principle that would prove practically workable and that also, as a practical matter, would help protect individuals against oppression. Thus, we can find in the Constitution's structural complexity an effort to produce a form of democracy that would prevent any single group of individuals from exercising too much power, thereby helping to protect an individual's (modern) fundamental liberty. And we can find in that structural complexity an effort to create a form of democratic government likely to escape those tendencies to produce the self-destructive public policies that the Pennsylvania and Massachusetts experiments had revealed, a form of democratic government that could produce legislation that would match the needs of the nation.

Consider, for example, what James Madison called the problem of "faction." As described by Gordon Wood, the problem grew out of the fact that the new nation encompassed divergent social, economic, and religious interests. There were "rich and poor; creditors and debtors; a landed interest, a monied interest, a mercantile interest, a manufacturing interest" and numerous subdivisions within each category. The states' post-revolutionary experience demonstrated that the natural tendency of these groups was to choose representatives not for their "abilities, integrity, or patriotism" but for their willingness to act solely to advance the group's particular interests. This often meant that "the great objects" of society were "sacrificed constantly to local views." The unicameral state legislatures, with their small electoral districts, large numbers of seats, and annual terms, might have come close to the Athenian vision of true democracy. But these bodies were "bulging and fluctuating" and "filled with such narrow-minded politicians who constantly mistook 'the particular circle' in which they moved for the 'general voice' of society." The Framers' goal was to "secure the public good and private rights against the danger of [factionalism], and at the same time to preserve the spirit and form of popular government." [18]

How did they achieve that goal? Madison said that the answer was to broaden the electoral base so that more members of government owe their position to the many. "If elected officials were concerned with only the interest of those who elected them, then their outlook was most easily broadened by enlarging their electorate." The base could not be made too broad, to the point where the elected official loses contact with the voter. But it must be broad enough to stifle the propensity "to rash measures and the facility of forming and executing them." It must be broad enough so that "no one common interest or passion will be likely to unite a majority of the whole number in an unjust pursuit." Madison predicted that this broadening would also have the effect of drawing out "representatives whose enlightened views and virtuous sentiments render them superior to local prejudices and to schemes of injustice" and more likely to pursue the true interests of the nation. What is more, a bicameral legislature would prevent usurpation of the people's ultimate power by forcing designing men to control two houses instead of one and by dividing the "trust" of the people between "different bodies of men, who might watch and check each other." [19]

Consistent with Madison's analysis, the Constitution provides that a House member's electoral district will remain small whereas a senator's district and the President's district will encompass the entire state and the entire nation respectively. The larger districts, by including many diverse interests, lessen the likelihood that a particular faction will win influence at the expense of the general well-being of a constituency's citizens. Moreover, House members can serve only two-year terms and need be only twenty-five years old, but senators serve for six years and must be thirty. The President, though serving for four years, must be thirty-five. The longer the terms of office and the older the minimum required age, the greater the insulation from short-term caprice of public sentiment and the more likely the elected official would be a proven leader rather than an untested political heir. At the same time, senators and the President would remain responsible to the people through election, by state legislators or through the Electoral College.[20]

Consider, too, the way in which the Constitution's original structure helped to protect the individual from oppressive governmental action, an objective as important to the early Americans as was the need to assure that the federal government's powers sprang from, and that it was accountable to, the people. Many, initially, had denied any possible conflict between the goals, for they believed that a thoroughly democratic government based on public liberty would naturally protect the individual rights of its citizens. They thought that securing "the right of the people to participate" in the government was the best way to secure the modern liberty of individuals. But the state government experiments in less disciplined democracy had proved disappointing in this respect as well, bringing about what some called a new form of despotism.[21]

Thus, the Constitution contains structural safeguards. One set of safeguards consists of a complex structure with checks and balances among federal branches, along with delegation to the federal government of limited powers, which diffused power and prevented impetuous action by the central government. One could understand an independent judiciary as providing additional protection, for judges could interpret the Constitution's delegation of limited powers to the federal government as excluding the authority to take action that deprived individual citizens of their (negative) liberty. State constitutions added further protections to curb the excesses of state government. But many of those who wrote and ratified the Constitution believed that neither the "liberty of the ancients" alone nor that liberty embodied in a complex constitutional structure would prove sufficient. And they added a Bill of Rights—the Constitution's first ten amendments—with explicit protections against government interference with certain fundamental personal liberties (including freedom of speech, of religion, and of the press).

The important point is that history permits me to answer affirmatively my original question: namely, historically speaking can one reasonably view the Constitution as focused upon democratic self-government? The answer is that from a historical perspective, one can reasonably view the Constitution as focusing upon active liberty, both as important in itself and as a partial means to help secure individual (modern) freedom. The Framers included elements designed to "control and mitigate" the ill effects of more direct forms of democratic government, but in doing so, the Framers "did not see themselves as repudiating either the Revolution or popular government." Rather, they were "saving both from their excesses." The act of ratifying the Constitution, by means of special state elections with broad voter eligibility rules, signaled the democratic character of the document itself.[22]

As history has made clear, the original Constitution was insufficient. It did not include a majority of the nation within its "democratic community." It took a civil war and eighty years of racial segregation before the slaves and their descendants could begin to think of the Constitution as theirs. Nor did women receive the right to vote until 1920. The "people" had to amend the Constitution, not only to extend its democratic base but also to expand and more fully to secure basic individual (modern) liberty.

But the original document sowed the democratic seed. Madison described something fundamental about American government, then and now, when he said the Constitution is a "charter...of power...granted by liberty," not (as in Europe) a "charter of liberty...granted by power."[23] He described a public creed when, in *Federalist* Number 39, he said:

> It is evident that no other form [of government] would be reconcilable with the genius of the people of America; with the fundamental principles of the Revolution; or with that honorable determination which animates every votary of freedom to rest all our political experiments on the capacity of mankind for self-government.[24]

For present purposes this description will suffice. It supports a certain view of the original Constitution's primary objective. That view sees the Constitution as furthering active liberty, as creating a form of government in which all citizens share the government's authority, participating in the creation of public policy. It understands the Constitution's structural complexity as responding to certain practical needs, for delegation, for nondestructive (and hopefully sound) public policies, and for protection of basic individual freedoms. And it views the Constitution's democratic imperative as accommodating, even insisting upon, these practical needs. Later amendments to a degree transformed the Constitution; but in doing so, they also confirmed and perfected underlying constitutional goals that, in part, were already there.

In sum, our constitutional history has been a quest for workable government, workable democratic government, workable democratic government protective of individual personal liberty. Our central commitment has been to "government of the people, by the people, for the people." And the applications following illustrate how this constitutional understanding helps interpret the Constitution—in a way that helps to resolve problems related to *modern* government.

A definition of the concept of "active liberty"
The concept of active liberty—as I said at the outset—refers to a sharing of a nation's sovereign authority

among its people. Sovereignty involves the legitimacy of a governmental action. And a sharing of sovereign authority suggests several kinds of connection between that legitimacy and the people.

For one thing, it should be possible to trace, without much difficulty, a line of authority for the making of governmental decisions back to the people themselves— either directly, or indirectly through those whom the people have chosen, perhaps instructed, to make certain kinds of decisions in certain ways. And this authority must be broad. The people must have room to decide and leeway to make mistakes.

For another, the people themselves should participate in government—though their participation may vary in degree. Participation is most forceful when it is direct, involving, for example, voting, town meetings, political party membership, or issue- or interest-related activities. It is weak, but still minimally exists, to the extent that it is vicarious, reflected, say, in the understanding that each individual belongs to the political community with the right to participate should he or she choose to do so.

Finally, the people, and their representatives, must have the capacity to exercise their democratic responsibilities. They should possess the tools, such as information and education, necessary to participate and to govern effectively.

When I refer to active liberty, I mean to suggest connections of this kind between the people and their

Active Liberty

government—connections that involve responsibility, participation, and capacity. Moreover, active liberty cannot be understood in a vacuum, for it operates in the real world. And in the real world, institutions and methods of interpretation must be designed in a way such that this form of liberty is both sustainable over time and capable of translating the people's will into sound policies.

Active liberty as a "theme" of constitutional interpretation

In discussing "active liberty"—a theme that resonates throughout the Constitution—I hope to illustrate how such a theme can affect a judge's interpretation of a constitutional text.[25] To illustrate a theme is not to present a general theory of constitutional interpretation. Nonetheless, themes play an important role in a judge's work. The great American twentieth century judge, Learned Hand, once compared the task of interpreting a statute to that of interpreting a musical score. No particular theory guarantees that the interpreter can fully capture the composer's intent. It makes sense to ask a musician to emphasize one theme more than another. And one can understand an interpretation that approaches a great symphony from a "romantic," as opposed to a "classical," point of view. So might a judge pay greater attention to a document's democratic theme; and so might a judge view the Constitution through a more democratic lens. The matter is primarily one of approach, perspective, and emphasis. And approach, perspective, and emphasis, even if they are not theories, play a great role in law.[26]

For one thing, emphasis matters when judges are presented with difficult questions of statutory or constitutional interpretation. All judges use similar basic tools to help them accomplish the task. They read the text's language along with related language in other parts of the document. They take account of its history, including history that shows what the language likely meant to those who wrote it. They look to tradition indicating how the relevant language was, and is, used in the law. They examine precedents interpreting the phrase, holding or suggesting what the phrase means and how it has been applied. They try to understand the phrase's purposes or (in respect of many constitutional phrases) the values that it embodies, and they consider the likely consequences of the interpretive alternatives, valued in terms of the phrase's purposes. But the fact that most judges agree that these basic elements—language, history, tradition, precedent, purpose, and consequence—are useful does not mean they agree about just where and how to use them. Some judges emphasize the use of language, history, and tradition. Others emphasize purpose and consequence. These differences of emphasis matter—and this book will explain why.

For another thing, emphasis matters in respect to the specialized constitutional work of a Supreme Court Justice. In my view, that work, though appellate in nature, differs from the work of a lower appellate court in an important way. Because a Justice, unlike a judge on a trial or appellate court, faces a steady diet of constitutional cases, Supreme Court work leads the Justice to develop a view of the Constitution as a whole. My own view is likely similar to that of others insofar as I see the document as creating a coherent framework for a certain kind of government. Described generally, that government is democratic; it avoids concentration of too much power in too few hands; it protects personal liberty; it insists that the law respect each individual equally; and it acts only upon the basis of law itself. The document embodies these general objectives in discrete provisions. In respect to democratic government, for example, the Constitution insists that Congress meet at least once each year, that elections take place every two (or four or six) years, that representation be based upon a census that must take place every decade; and it has gradually extended the right to vote to all adult men and women of every race and religion. (It also guarantees the states a "republican form of government.")[27]

But my view can differ from the views of various others in the way in which I understand the relation between the Constitution's democratic objective and its other general objectives. My view can differ in the comparative significance I attach to each general objective. And my view can differ in the way I understand how a particular objective should influence the interpretation of a broader provision, and not just those provisions that refer to it directly. These differences, too, are often a matter of degree, a matter of perspective, or emphasis, rather than a radical disagreement about the general nature of the Constitution or its basic objectives.

Finally, the fact that members of historically different Supreme Courts have emphasized different constitutional themes, objectives, or approaches over time allows us to characterize a Court during a period of its history and to speak meaningfully about changes in the Court's judicial "philosophy" over time. Thus, one can characterize the early nineteenth century as a period during which the Court, through its interpretations of the Constitution, helped to establish the authority of the federal government, including the federal judiciary. One can characterize the late nineteenth and early twentieth centuries as a period during which the Court overly emphasized the Constitution's protection of private property, as, for example, in *Lochner v. New York,* where (over the dissent of Justice Oliver Wendell Holmes) it held that state maximum hour laws violated "freedom of contract" which right it found "implicit" in the Constitution. At the same time, that Court wrongly underemphasized the basic objectives of the Civil War amendments (abolishing slavery, guaranteeing equal protection of the laws, and forbidding denial of the right to vote on account of race). It tended to ignore that those amendments sought to draw all citizens, irrespective of race, into the community, and

Active Liberty

that those amendments, in guaranteeing that the law would equally respect all "persons," hoped to make the Constitution's opening phrase, "We the People," a political reality.[28]

Later Courts—the New Deal Court in the 1930s and 1940s and the Warren Court in the 1950s and 1960s—emphasized ways in which the Constitution protected the citizen's "active liberty," i.e., the scope of the right to participate in government. The former dismantled various *Lochner*-era distinctions, thereby expanding the constitutional room available for citizens, through their elected representatives, to govern themselves. The latter interpreted the Civil War amendments in light of their basic purposes, thereby directly helping African Americans become full members of the nation's community of self-governing citizens—a community that the people had expanded through later amendments, for example, those extending the suffrage to women, and which the Court expanded further in its "one person, one vote" decisions. The Warren Court's emphasis (on the need to make the law's constitutional promises a legal reality) also led it to consider how the Civil War amendments (and later amendments) had changed the scope of pre–Civil War constitutional language, that is, by changing the assumptions, premises, or presuppositions upon which many earlier constitutional interpretations had rested. In doing so, it read the document as offering broader protection to "modern liberty" (protecting the citizen from government) as well. While I cannot easily characterize the current Court, I will suggest that it may have swung back too far, too often underemphasizing or overlooking the contemporary importance of active liberty.[29]

The book's objective

I hope by now to have convinced the reader that, when a judge seeks to interpret the Constitution, themes, approaches, and matters of emphasis can make a difference. This book will describe one such theme, that of active liberty. I shall show, through a set of six examples (focused on contemporary problems), how increased emphasis upon that theme can help judges interpret constitutional and statutory provisions. The examples are drawn from the areas of free speech, federalism, privacy, equal protection, statutory interpretation, and judicial review of administrative action. Each example considers modern government-related problems that call for a democratically based response. And each raises difficult questions of constitutional or statutory interpretation. In each instance I believe that increased recognition of the Constitution's democratic objective can help judges deal more effectively with interpretive issues, thereby helping communities deal better with the problems that have called those issues into being.

After illustrating how use of the democratic theme can help judges better interpret constitutional and statutory provisions, I shall link use of the theme to a broader interpretive approach that places considerable importance upon consequences; and I shall contrast that approach with others that place greater weight upon language, history, and tradition. In the process, I hope to illustrate the work of a judge of a constitutional court; to justify use of the general interpretive approach I implicitly set forth; to explain why I believe that a different interpretive approach that undervalues consequences, by undervaluing related constitutional objectives, exacts a constitutional price that is too high; to focus increased attention upon the Constitution's democratic objective; and, in doing so, to promote reemphasis of those objectives as an important theme that significantly helps judges interpret the Constitution.

CHAPTER TWO

FREEDOM OF SPEECH

The first example focuses on the First Amendment and how it applies if the government seeks to regulate certain activities affecting speech, in particular campaign finance, corporate advertising about matters of public concern, and drugstore advertising informing the public that custom-made pharmaceuticals are available. These examples show the importance of reading the First Amendment not in isolation but as seeking to maintain a system of free expression designed to further a basic constitutional purpose: creating and maintaining democratic decision-making institutions.

The example begins where courts normally begin in First Amendment cases. They try to classify the speech at issue, distinguishing among different speech-related activities for the purpose of applying a strict, moderately strict, or totally relaxed presumption of unconstitutionality. Is the speech "political speech," calling for a strong pro-speech presumption, "commercial speech," calling for a mid-range presumption, or simply a form of economic regulation presumed constitutional?

Should courts begin in this way? Some argue that making these kinds of categorical distinctions is a misplaced enterprise. The Constitution's language makes no such distinction. It simply protects "the freedom of speech" from government restriction. "Speech is speech and that is the end of the matter." But to limit distinctions to the point at which First Amendment law embodies the slogan "speech is speech" cannot work. And the fact that the First Amendment seeks to protect active liberty as well as modern liberty helps to explain why.[1]

The democratic government that the Constitution creates now regulates a host of activities that inevitably take place through the medium of speech. Today's workers manipulate information, not wood or metal. And the modern information-based workplace, no less than its more materially based predecessors, requires the application of community standards seeking to assure, for example, the absence of anti-competitive restraints; the accuracy of information; the absence of discrimination; the protection of health, safety, the environment, the consumer; and so forth.

Laws that embody these standards obviously affect speech. Warranty laws require private firms to include on labels statements of specified content. Securities laws and consumer protection laws insist upon the disclosure of information that businesses might prefer to keep private. Health laws forbid tobacco advertising, say, to children. Anti-discrimination laws insist that employers prevent employees from making certain kinds of statements. Communications laws require cable broadcasters to provide network access. Campaign finance laws restrict citizen contributions to candidates.

To treat all these instances alike, to scrutinize them all as if they all represented a similar kind of legislative effort to restrain a citizen's "modern liberty" to speak, would lump together too many different kinds of activities under the aegis of a single standard, thereby creating a dilemma. On the one hand, if strong First Amendment standards were to apply across the board, they would prevent a democratically elected government from creating necessary regulation. The strong free speech guarantees needed to protect the structural democratic governing process, if applied without distinction to all governmental efforts to control speech, would unreasonably limit the public's substantive economic (or social) regulatory choices. The limits on substantive choice would likely exceed what any liberty-protecting framework for democratic government could require, depriving the people of the democratically necessary room to make decisions, including the leeway to make regulatory mistakes. That, along with a singular lack of modesty, was the failing of *Lochner*. No one wants to replay that discredited history in modern First Amendment guise.

On the other hand, to apply across the board uniform First Amendment standards weak enough to avoid the shoals of *Lochner* would undermine the First Amendment so much that it would not offer sufficient protection for the free exchange of ideas necessary to maintain the health of our democracy. Most scholars, including "speech is speech" advocates, consequently see a need for distinctions. The question is, Which ones? Applied where? At this point, reference to the Constitution's more general objectives helps. First, active liberty is particularly at risk when law restricts speech directly related to the shaping of public opinion, for example, speech that takes place in areas related to politics and policy-making by elected officials. That special risk justifies especially strong pro-speech judicial presumptions. It also justifies careful review whenever the speech in question seeks to shape public opinion, particularly if that opinion in turn will affect the political process and the kind of society in which we live.

Second, whenever ordinary commercial or economic regulation is at issue, this special risk normally is absent. Moreover, strong pro-speech presumptions risk imposing what is, from the perspective of active liberty, too severe a restriction upon the legislature—a restriction that would dramatically limit the size of the legislative arena that the Constitution opens for public deliberation and action. The presence of this second risk warns against use of special, strong pro-speech judicial presumptions or special regulation-skeptical judicial review.

The upshot is that reference to constitutional purposes in general and active liberty in particular helps to justify the category of review that the Court applies to a given type of law. But those same considerations argue, among other things, against category boundaries that are too rigid or fixed and against too mechanical an application of those categories. Rather, reference to active liberty will help courts define and apply the categories case by case.

Consider campaign finance reform. The campaign finance problem arises out of the explosion of campaign costs, particularly those related to television advertising, together with the vast disparity in ability to make a campaign contribution. In the year 2000, for example, election expenditures amounted to $1.4 billion, and the two presidential candidates spent about $310 million. In 2002, an off-year without a presidential contest, campaign expenditures still amounted to more than $1 billion. A typical House election cost $900,000, with an open seat costing $1.2 million; a typical Senate seat cost about $4.8 million, with an open contested seat costing about $7.1 million.[2]

Comparable expenditures in foreign democracies are far lower. A typical British or Canadian parliamentary election involves expenditures for individual seats of about $13,000 and $43,000 respectively. (Television costs explain much of the difference. The cost of television advertising in the United States now approximates $10,000 per minute in a major city. In the 2000 election, parties and candidates spent between $770 million and $1 billion on television ads. Other nations provide limited television time to candidates at reduced rates or free of charge.)[3]

A small number of individuals and groups underwrite a very large share of these costs. In 2000, about half the money the parties spent, roughly $500 million, was soft money, i.e., money not subject to regulation under the then current campaign finance laws. Two-thirds of that money—almost $300 million—came from just 800 donors, each contributing a minimum of $120,000. Of these donors, 435 were corporations or unions (whose *direct* contributions the law forbids). The rest, 365, were individual citizens. At the same time, 99 per cent of the 200 million or so citizens eligible to vote gave less than $200. Ninety-six per cent gave nothing at all.[4]

The upshot is a concern, reflected in campaign finance laws, that the few who give in large amounts may have special access to, and therefore influence over, their elected representatives or, at least, create the appearance of undue influence. (One study found, for example, that 55 per cent of Americans believe that large contributions have a "great deal" of impact on how decisions are made in Washington; fewer than 1 per cent believed they had no impact.) These contributions (particularly if applied to television) may eliminate the need for, and in that sense crowd out, smaller individual contributions. In either case, the public may lose confidence in the political system and become less willing to participate in the political process. That, in important part, is why legislatures have tried to regulate the size of campaign contributions.[5]

Our Court, in 1976, considered the constitutionality of the congressional legislation that initially regulated campaign contributions, and in 2003 we considered more recent legislation that tried to close what Congress considered a loophole—the ability to make contributions in the form of unregulated soft money. The basic constitutional question does not concern the desirability or wisdom of the legislation but whether, how, and the extent to which, the First Amendment permits the legislature to impose limits on the amounts that individuals or organizations or parties can contribute to a campaign. Here it is possible to sketch an approach to decision-making that draws upon the Constitution's democratic objective.[6]

It is difficult to find an easy answer to this basic constitutional question in language, in history, or in tradition. The First Amendment's language says that Congress shall not abridge "the freedom of speech." But it does not define "the freedom of speech" in any detail. The nation's Founders did not speak directly about campaign contributions. Madison, who decried faction, thought that Members of Congress would fairly represent all their constituents, in part because the "electors" would not be the "rich" any more than the "poor." But this kind of statement, while modestly helpful to the cause of campaign finance reform, is far from determinative.[7]

Neither can we find the answer through the use of purely conceptual arguments. Some claim, for example, that "money is speech." Others say, "money is not speech."

But neither contention helps. Money is not speech, it is money. But the expenditure of money enables speech, and that expenditure is often necessary to communicate a message, particularly in a political context. A law that forbade the expenditure of money to communicate could effectively suppress the message.

Nor does it resolve the problem simply to point out that campaign contribution limits inhibit the political "speech opportunities" of those who wish to contribute more. Indeed, that is so. But the question is whether, in context, such a limitation is prohibited as an abridgment of "the freedom of speech." To announce that the harm imposed by a contribution limit is under no circumstances justified is simply to state an ultimate constitutional conclusion; it is not to explain the underlying reasons.[8]

Once we remove our blinders, however, paying increased attention to the Constitution's general democratic objective, it becomes easier to reach a solution. To understand the First Amendment as seeking in significant part to protect active liberty, "participatory self-government," is to understand it as protecting more than the individual's modern freedom. It is to understand the amendment as seeking to facilitate a conversation among ordinary citizens that will encourage their informed participation in the electoral process. It is to suggest a constitutional purpose that goes beyond protecting the individual from government restriction of information about matters that the Constitution commits

to individual, not collective, decision-making. It is to understand the First Amendment as seeking primarily to encourage the exchange of information and ideas necessary for citizens themselves to shape that "public opinion which is the final source of government in a democratic state." In these ways the Amendment helps to maintain a form of government open to participation (in Constant's words) by "all the citizens, without exception." [9]

To focus upon the First Amendment's relation to the Constitution's democratic objective is helpful because the campaign laws seek to further a similar objective. They seek to democratize the influence that money can bring to bear upon the electoral process, thereby building public confidence in that process, broadening the base of a candidate's meaningful financial support, and encouraging greater public participation. Ultimately, they seek thereby to maintain the integrity of the political process—a process that itself translates political speech into governmental action. In so far as they achieve these objectives, those laws, despite the limits they impose, will help to further the kind of open public political discussion that the First Amendment seeks to sustain, both as an end and as a means of achieving a workable democracy.

To emphasize the First Amendment's protection of active liberty is not to find the campaign finance laws automatically constitutional. Rather, it is to recognize that basic democratic objectives, including some of a kind that the First Amendment seeks to further, lie on both sides of the constitutional equation. Seen in terms of modern liberty, they include protection of the citizen's speech from government interference; seen in terms of active liberty, they include promotion of a democratic conversation. That, I believe, is why our Court has refused to apply a strong First Amendment presumption that would almost automatically find the laws unconstitutional. Rather the Court has consistently rejected "strict scrutiny" as the proper test, instead of examining a campaign finance law "close[ly]" while applying what it calls "heightened" scrutiny. In doing so, the Court has emphasized the power of large campaign contributions to "erod[e] public confidence in the electoral process." It has noted that contribution limits are "aimed at protecting the integrity of the process"; pointed out that, in doing so, they "tangibly benefit public participation in political debate"; and concluded that that is why "there is no place for the strong presumption against constitutionality, of the sort often thought to accompany the words 'strict scrutiny.' " In this statement it recognizes the possibility that, just as a restraint of trade is sometimes lawful because it furthers, rather than restricts, competition, so a restriction on speech, even when political speech is at issue, will sometimes prove reasonable, hence lawful. Consequently the Court has tried to look realistically both at a campaign finance law's *negative* impact upon those primarily wealthier citizens who wish to engage in more electoral communication and its *positive* impact upon the public's confidence in,

and ability to communicate through, the electoral process. And it has applied a constitutional test that I would
describe as one of proportionality. Does the statute strike
a reasonable balance between electoral speech-restricting
and speech-enhancing consequences? Or does it instead
impose restrictions on speech that are disproportionate
when measured against their electoral and speech-related
benefits, taking into account the kind, the importance,
and the extent of those benefits, as well as the need for the
restriction in order to secure them?[10]

In trying to answer these questions, courts need not
totally abandon what I have referred to as judicial modesty. Courts can defer to the legislature's own judgement
in so far as that judgment concerns matters (particularly
empirical matters) about which the legislature is comparatively expert, such as the extent of the campaign
finance problem, a matter that directly concerns the
realities of political life. But courts should not defer when
they evaluate the risk that reform legislation will defeat
the participatory self-government objective itself. That
risk is present, for example, when laws set contribution
limits so low that they elevate the reputation-related or
media-related advantages of incumbency to the point
of insulating incumbent officeholders from effective
challenge.[11]

A focus upon the Constitution's democratic objective
does not offer easy answers to the difficult questions that
campaign finance laws pose. But it does clarify the First

Amendment's role in promoting active liberty and suggests an approach for addressing those and other vexing questions. In turn, such a focus can help the Court arrive at answers faithful to the Constitution, its language, and its parts, read together as a consistent whole. Modesty suggests when, and how, courts should defer to the legislature in doing so.

The inquiry is complex. But courts both here and abroad have engaged in similarly complex inquiries when the constitutionality of electoral laws is at issue. That complexity is demanded by a Constitution that grants to Congress the power to secure a fair electoral system while requiring judges to conduct First Amendment review of Congress's decisions.

Reference to the Constitution's "participatory self-government" goal helps resolve other kinds of First Amendment problems as well, for example, those raised by commercial speech such as commercial advertising. To what extent does the First Amendment protect that speech from government regulation?

Several recent cases have focused upon the question. In one of them the Court considered a California law that, as interpreted, allowed any member of the public to bring a "deceptive business practices" claim against a corporation that had advertised (and distributed to other potential customers) its denials of charges that it was engaging in disreputable business practices abroad. The California court upheld the law, and ultimately our Court refused review for procedural reasons.[12]

In another, the Court struck down a law forbidding pharmacists to advertise the availability of individual "compound drugs," prescription drugs that the pharmacist makes up specially for patients with unique requirements (say, because of drug-related allergies). The Court said that the First Amendment forbids statutory effort to restrict information in order to help the public make wiser decisions. The Court thought the pharmacy law was just such an effort.[13]

In each case I disagreed. I wrote in my dissent that the business practice speech was primarily political and not subject to regulation. I thought that the pharmacist's speech was primarily commercial and subject to regulation. If the Court had seen active liberty as the moving force behind the creation of, and application of, the First Amendment's categorical distinctions, then these cases might have come out differently.[14]

In the business practices case, Nike, a business corporation, tried to defend itself against claims by newspapers, human rights groups, and labor organizations that it had maintained inhumane working conditions and engaged in other disreputable business practices abroad. Nike denied these claims in letters sent to newspapers, to college athletic directors, and to others. The California Supreme Court permitted a private citizen to sue Nike for false advertising—on the ground that Nike's denials were themselves false. And that court found that the First Amendment gave Nike no particularly strong protection against such a lawsuit. Our Court initially decided to consider whether that decision was correct, but because of certain procedural difficulties, it ultimately dismissed the claim without reaching the merits. I did not agree with the Court's procedural conclusions, and I would have reversed the California Supreme Court, which had denied strong First Amendment protection to Nike's responses.[15]

In the pharmacy case, Congress forbade pharmacists to advertise specific compound drugs because those drugs had not been tested. While doctors would know of their existence and could prescribe them when necessary, advertising would generate strong patient demand, leading doctors to prescribe a given untested compound for patients for whom it was only a convenience, not a necessity. The law, in permitting prescriptions but forbidding advertising to consumers, struck a compromise between the patient's special need for drug compounds and the special risk of harm due to the fact that compound drugs (being individualized and special) had not met ordinary safety testing requirements.[16]

The Court majority thought that any subsequently created safety risk could not justify a law that, in the Court's view, reflected a "fear" that "people would make bad decisions if given truthful information about compounded drugs." But, for the reasons I have set forth when discussing "speech is speech," that omnipresent function—providing information—is not by itself sufficient to warrant a strong anti-regulatory presumption. And without such a presumption, the existence of widespread prescription drug advertising, the medical belief that "direct-to-consumer advertising pressures physicians into prescribing drugs they would not ordinarily prescribe," and the small but definite safety risk present in untested drugs together would have justified the "information restricting" law at issue.[17]

From the perspective of a First Amendment that seeks first and foremost to facilitate democratic self-government, the two courts' results in these two cases seem backwards. Nike responded to criticisms of its labor practices. Those criticisms lie at the center of an important public debate in which participants urge or oppose public collective action. Nike's speech sought to shape related public opinion. It sought to do so under the permissive legal standards that govern speech of its opponents. If the "false advertising" lawsuit goes forward, Nike (and other potential speakers), out of reasonable caution or even an excess of caution, might well censor their own expression significantly beyond what the law could constitutionally demand. What could be more central to basic First Amendment concerns?

The pharmacists' speech, by contrast, did not directly serve any such democratic purpose. The pharmacists did not seek through price advertising to contribute to a public debate about the relative merits of compound drugs. At most, they conveyed information that would help patients make more informed private decisions about what drugs to ask their physicians to prescribe. But this purpose, while important, is not so important that it justifies striking down legislation that regulates speech for sound reasons related to the traditional regulation of public health and safety. A contrary view of the First Amendment standard here fails to further, indeed it impedes, the workings of a democratically determined economic regulatory system. It restricts Congress's regulatory powers, preventing the public from achieving related objectives that the community democratically determines to be important.

I do not mean that the First Amendment leaves Congress free to enact any regulatory law it wishes related to commercial speech or to economic regulation. Traditional modern liberty—the individual's freedom from government restriction—remains important. Individuals need information freely to make decisions about their own lives. And, irrespective of context, a particular rule affecting speech might, in a particular instance, require individuals to act against conscience, inhibit public debate, threaten artistic expression, censor views in ways unrelated to a program's basic objectives, or create other risks of abuse. These possibilities themselves form the raw material out of which courts will create different presumptions applicable in different speech contexts. And even in the absence of presumptions, courts will examine individual instances with the possibilities of such harms in mind.

My argument is that, in applying First Amendment presumptions, we must distinguish among areas, contexts, and forms of speech. Reference to basic constitutional purposes can help generate the relevant distinctions. And reference back to at least one general purpose, active liberty, helps both to generate proper distinctions and also properly to apply the distinctions generated. The active liberty reference helps us to preserve speech that is essential to our democratic form of government, while simultaneously permitting the law to deal effectively with such modern regulatory problems as campaign finance and product or workplace safety.

CHAPTER THREE

FEDERALISM

The next example concerns recent Court cases that bring into focus federalism and its relationship to two general questions of modern government. First, how can we reconcile democratic decision-making with the highly technical nature of many government decisions? Second, what level of government is best suited to the making of which decisions? I cannot provide a general answer to these questions. But I can suggest that, by taking explicit account of the Constitution's liberty-related objectives, judicial decisions will help the three branches of government together arrive at better answers.

It is important to understand that the word "federalism," in American constitutional discussions often refers to the rights of the States, i.e., the Constitution's guarantees that assure the retention by the States of particular powers. In European discussion, however, the same word may be used to refer to a delegation of power from, say the Member States of the European Union. Since the word describes a particular kind of relationship between a central government and its constituent parts, one can emphasize either aspect. Here I shall emphasize the State's retained powers.

Active Liberty

When one focuses upon the Constitution's efforts to maintain State authority by creating a federal structure, it becomes clear that such a structure helps to protect modern liberty. A division of powers among federal and state governments makes it more difficult for the federal government to tell state and local governments what they must do. And it thereby frees citizens from restraints that a more distant central government might otherwise impose. Yet it leaves citizens subject to similar restraints imposed by the states themselves. Thus it seems more natural to view the structure as helping to secure more effective forms of *active* liberty, i.e., as facilitating meaningful citizen participation in government by preserving a more local decision-making process.

My colleague Justice Sandra Day O'Connor has explained the connections well. By guaranteeing state and local government's broad decision-making authority, federalist principles secure decisions that rest on knowledge of local circumstances, help to develop a sense of shared purposes and commitments among local citizens, and ultimately facilitate "novel social and economic experiments." Through increased transparency, those principles make it easier for citizens to hold government officials accountable. And by bringing government closer to home, they help maintain a sense of local community. In all these ways they facilitate and encourage the ancient liberty that Constant described: citizen participation in the government's decision-making process.[1]

Today, this participation principle must be implemented against the backdrop of a highly complex set of technology-based social problems that defy decision purely at local or purely at federal levels. Rather, they call for a federal-state cooperation that permits effective action while respecting the liberty I have just described.

Consider the regulation of toxic chemicals. Some toxic chemical regulation must take place at the national level. Chemical substances, traveling through air, water, or soil, often affect the environment in more than one state. Chemical substance regulation demands scientific and technical expertise often more readily available at the federal level. Federal regulation, because it is national in scope, can facilitate the development of a national understanding about chemical dangers, say by promoting a simple, uniform language for talking about safety risks. And only a federal regulator can set minimum substantive standards designed to avoid a race to the bottom among states hoping to attract industry investment.

Yet some aspects of the problem would seem better regulated at a state or local level. Similar amounts of similar chemicals in air or water or soil may have different toxic effects depending upon local conditions. Similar emissions standards may have different economic effects depending upon differing economic circumstances in different communities. And different communities may place different weights upon similar clean-up (risk-reduction) benefits and costs. These differences suggest that citizens in different local communities may come up with different answers to the same basic questions: How clean should our local waste dump be? And at what cost?

The idea of "cooperative federalism" tries to provide regulatory answers that take account of these needs. Federal agencies no longer rely exclusively upon classical command-and-control regulation. They have supplemented that form of regulation with less restrictive, more incentive-based, methods, including special taxes and marketable rights. Federal agencies can make expertise available to state and local officials without imposing their will. Those agencies may help separate questions of common interest (particularly those that require expertise) from more locally oriented questions of fact or value. These approaches mean more decision-making authority for local governments; they place greater power in the hands of individuals; and, in doing so, they further the liberty interests—both active and modern—that underlie federalist principles.

To what extent have the Court's recent federalism decisions taken these considerations into account? Each Court holding helps to some degree to protect modern liberty—in the narrow sense described. That is to say, the decisions limit the federal government's ability to control the activities of individuals and businesses. But in respect to the furtherance of active liberty these decisions are often retrograde. They discourage use of the cooperative, incentive-based regulatory methods that I have just mentioned. Thus, in unanticipated ways, they paradoxically threaten to shift regulatory activity from the state and local to the federal level—the likely opposite of their objective.

Consider first the Court's holding that federalism means that Congress may not write laws that "commandeer" a state's legislative or executive officials. Thus, Congress cannot require a state legislature to write a particular kind of law, for example, a nuclear waste storage law. Nor can Congress enact a law that requires a local official to spend time enforcing a federal policy, for example, a law that requires a local sheriff to see whether a potential gun buyer has a criminal record. These interpretations of the Constitution's federalism requirements stop Congress from enlisting local officials to check compliance with federal minimum standards. They thereby force Congress either to forgo the program in question altogether or, perhaps more likely, to expand the size of the program-related federal enforcement bureaucracy. Other things being equal and given ordinary bureaucratic tendencies, this fact will make it harder, not easier, to shift regulatory power from the federal government to state and local governments. And it will make it harder, not easier, to experiment with incentive-based regulatory methods.[2]

Justice John Paul Stevens illustrated the problem. In a dissent, presciently written before the terrorist attacks of September 11, 2001, he wrote that the "threat of an international terrorist... may require a national response before federal personnel can be made available to respond.... [What in the Constitution] forbids the enlistment of state officials to make that response effective?" Would freedom to enlist state officials not help to advance both the cause of national security and the cause of cooperative federalism?[3]

Consider next the Court's decisions that have significantly limited Congress's power (under the Commerce Clause or the Fourteenth Amendment) to require a state to waive its Eleventh Amendment immunity from suit by private citizens. Judged in terms of their consequences, it is difficult to see how these decisions advance cooperative federalism. To the contrary, they make it more difficult for Congress to create uniform individual remedies under legislation dealing with nationwide problems— for example, private civil damages actions for citizens injured by a state's unlawful use of their intellectual property. Less obviously, but as importantly, they will prevent Congress from adopting certain forms of "less restrictive" regulation—forms that mean less federal government interference in state, local, or personal matters.[4]

Suppose, for example, that Congress, reluctant to expand a federal regulatory bureaucracy, sees citizen suits as a way to ensure that state entities (as well as private entities) comply with toxic waste dump legislation. Suppose that Congress, in an effort to achieve a particular environmental goal, directs state governments to impose environmental taxes and permits private citizens to sue a state to protest a particular tax assessment or to obtain a tax refund. Or suppose that Congress, anxious to shrink the size of, say, its federal maritime law enforcement staff, permits individual citizens to bring federal administrative proceedings against state port authorities, providing for federal enforcement only where administrative proceedings determine them to be justified. The Court's Eleventh Amendment decisions rule out these less restrictive, less bureaucratic methods of enforcing federal law—a consequence inconsistent with both modern freedom and the Constitution's vision of active liberty.[5]

Finally, consider cases in which the Court has limited the scope of Congress's Commerce Clause powers. The Court has found that gun possession near local schools and violence against women in local communities do not sufficiently "affect" interstate commerce to permit Congress to legislate. Decisions in this third category do mean less federal regulation. They do not directly discourage citizen participation in "incentive-based," or "cooperative" state-federal, regulatory programs. But in these instances the public has participated in the legislative process at the national level. Indeed, Congress held elaborate public hearings only to find its legislative work nullified.[6]

Moreover, these cases *indirectly* may discourage the development of complex cooperative programs. That is because the Court's own close scrutiny of, and reweighing of, the evidence that Congress found sufficient to show "interstate effects" create uncertainty about how much evidence is needed to find the constitutionally requisite effect. Certain portions of the Court's reasoning, such as its refusal to consider the "aggregate" effect on interstate commerce of individually small "non-economic" events, aggravate that uncertainty. Congress then may not know whether it can, or it cannot, legislate the details of a particular "cooperative"—federal, state, local—regulatory framework. And there is no speedy way for it to find out. Those circumstances, other things being equal, make it less likely that Congress will enact laws that might well embody cooperative federalist principles.[7]

The consequences that I have just described do not show that the Court's federalism decisions are wrong. (Though I believe they are wrong and that the Court was right in yet more recent cases to slow down, perhaps to halt, this development). The examples simply raise such questions as: why should courts try to answer difficult federalism questions on the basis of logical deduction from text or precedent alone? Why not ask about the consequences of decision-making on the active liberty that federalism seeks to further? Why not at least consider the practical effects on local democratic self-government of decisions interpreting the Constitution's principles of federalism—principles that themselves seek to further that very kind of government? Why remain willfully blind to one important dimension of the Constitution's federalism objective, that of active liberty?[8]

The examples also suggest a need for a better "dialogue" between Congress and the Court in this area. Judge-made law interpreting the dormant Commerce Clause foresees such a dialogue. That doctrine asks courts to decide, among other things, whether a state regulatory law unreasonably inhibits trade with other states. The doctrine weighs basic principles of federalism against local economic protectionism, a matter highly relevant in an increasingly global economy. Does a state law that, for example, prohibits importing peaches grown with certain pesticides, insists on the use of special steel for elevator cables, or prevents interstate trucks from transporting dynamite during daylight hours, reasonably protect the state's citizens from dangerous pesticides, faulty elevators, and risks of explosion? Or does it unreasonably protect the state's peach growers, steelmakers, and contractors from out-of-state competition?[9]

In this area of constitutional "federalism" law, Congress is free to overturn by statute a judicial decision with which it disagrees. Congress can even delegate the power to decide such matters to an expert agency. The federal Department of Transportation, for example, after providing opportunity for public comment, can decide many "dormant Commerce Clause" questions subject only to judicial review of the reasonableness of its decision. The doctrine, while facilitating the use of expert opinion, thereby permits the public, acting through its elected representatives, to have the last word. It encourages judicial modesty in enforcing Commerce Clause objectives, leading courts to defer to the conclusions of the democratic process.[10]

The Court might also consider specific legal doctrines that would promote a similar dialogue in respect to federalism more generally. Through a hard-look requirement, for example, the Court would communicate to Congress the precise constitutional difficulty the Court has with the statute at issue without resorting to permanent invalidation. Congress, in reenacting the statute, would revisit the matter and respond to the Court's concerns. A clear-statement rule would have the Court call upon Congress to provide an unambiguous articulation of the precise contours and reach of a given policy solution. Those doctrines would lead the Court to focus upon the thoroughness of the legislature's consideration of a matter, thereby encouraging public participation, and the explicit nature of its conclusion, thereby promoting clarity and consequent accountability. As their names suggest, they would require Congress to look hard at and speak clearly on a matter, but they rarely would create an absolute "federalism-based" bar to legislation. Such an approach treads carefully and with restraint when courts consider the validity of a legislative enactment, and it is consequently consistent with a Constitution that emphasizes active liberty.[11]

I am not arguing here the question of whether the Constitution permits development of these kinds of legal doctrines. Rather, I am pointing to the Constitution's democratic objectives, explaining the complexity involved in attaining those objectives when modern technical decision-making is at issue, noting the related tension between those objectives and the recent cases, and suggesting that proper resolution of many such federalism issues cannot be left to the judiciary alone. There are likely better ways.

CHAPTER FOUR
THE RIGHT OF PRIVACY

The third example concerns privacy. By privacy, I mean a person's power to control what others can come to know about him or her. It illustrates constitutional decision-making under conditions of uncertainty—uncertainty brought about by rapid changes in technology. Whenever technological advance means significant change in the regulatory environment, Americans normally search pragmatically for new legal answers, and they often participate in a democratic conversation along the way. Judicial respect for this process often counsels a special degree of judicial caution.

To explain the constitutional matter, I must begin by describing the privacy-related legal problem. I believe that this problem arises out of three factors: the variety of values implicated by our concern for privacy; the need for already complicated legal regimes to accommodate new technologies; and the difficulty of balancing competing (sometimes conflicting) concerns in this complex area of law.

First, an array of different values underlies the need to protect personal privacy from the "unwanted gaze." Some emphasize the values related to an individual's need to be left alone, not bothered by others, perhaps adding that privacy prevents us from being judged on the basis of a single preserved private fact taken out of context. Others emphasize the way in which important personal relationships, of love and friendship, depend upon trust, which, in turn, implies a sharing of information not available to all. Others find connections between personal privacy and individualism in that privacy may encourage nonconformity and more free expression. Still others, for similar reasons, find connections between privacy and equality; for example, an inability to obtain highly individualized information about customers can lead businesses to treat all customers alike. One might weigh these different considerations differently, but still almost everyone finds in them important relationships to an individual's dignity, and almost all Americans accept the need for legal rules to protect that dignity.[1]

Second, most of our privacy-related legal challenges lie at the intersection of a legal circumstance and a technological circumstance. The legal circumstance consists of the fact that several different types of laws are involved in regulating privacy. Some laws, such as trespass, wiretapping, eavesdropping, and search-and-seizure statutes, protect particular places or sites, such as homes or telephones, from searches and monitoring. Other laws protect not places but kinds of information, for example certain personal data, from access by another person. These different laws protect privacy to different degrees depending upon place, an individual's status, the type of information, and the kind of intrusion at issue.[2]

The technological circumstance consists of the fact that advancing technology has made the protective effects of present law uncertain, unpredictable, and incomplete. Video cameras now can monitor shopping malls, schools, parks, office buildings, city streets, and other places that current law had left unprotected. Scanners and interceptors can overhear virtually any electronic conversation. Thermal-imaging devices can detect from outside the home activities taking place within it. Technology now provides us with the ability to observe, collate, and permanently preserve a vast amount of information about individuals—information that the law previously did not prohibit people from collecting but which, in practice, was not readily collectible or easily preserved. These technological changes have altered the practical, privacy-related effect of the set of previously existing laws.

The legal circumstance and the technological circumstance taken together mean (1) a complex set of preexisting laws (2) applied in rapidly changing circumstances. That application means changed, perhaps diminished, privacy protection, with the *extent* to which protection diminishes varying depending upon individual circumstances. To maintain preexisting protection, we must look for new legal bottles to hold our old wine.

Third, revision of our laws affecting privacy requires balancing (not always agreed-upon) interests in a host of different areas of human activity in light of uncertain predictions about the technological future. The answer to the balancing question—how to balance the interests—is often far from clear.

Suppose, for example, that businesses using computers obtain detailed consumer purchasing information and create individualized customer profiles. Some believe that their possession of those profiles significantly diminishes the customer's privacy. But the profiles may also help firms provide products better tailored to fit customers' desires, and at lower costs.

Suppose, for example, that hospitals place an individual's medical records online. Doing so may compromise the patient's privacy. But the ready online availability of those records may also lower insurance costs or help a patient who arrives unconscious at an emergency room.

Suppose, for example, that the law insists that information about an individual's genetic make-up must remain confidential. That law will protect that individual's privacy. But what happens if a close relative, a nephew or cousin, needs that information to assess their own cancer risks?

It is tempting to think we can resolve these dilemmas simply by requiring that an individual whose privacy is threatened be informed and grant consent. But an "informed consent" requirement does not necessarily work. Consent forms can be signed without understanding. And, in any event, a decision by one individual to release information or to keep it confidential often affects the lives of others.

All of this is bound by what is technologically possible. Should the law require programming video cameras on public streets to turn off at certain times? When? Should the law require software that instructs computers to delete certain kinds of information? Which? Should the law require encrypted cell phones? Should the law impose upon certain websites a requirement that they permit users with certain privacy preferences to negotiate access-related privacy conditions? How? When will the software be available?

It is difficult even to begin to understand the legal, technological, and value-balancing complexity involved in trying to resolve the legal aspects of the personal privacy problem. I cannot offer solutions. But I can suggest how twenty-first-century Americans go about finding solutions. The way they do so is best described as a form of participatory democracy.

Ideally, in America, the lawmaking process does not involve legislators, administrators, or judges imposing law from above. Rather, it involves changes that bubble up from below. Serious complex legal change is often made in the context of a national conversation involving, among others, scientists, engineers, businessmen and women, the media, along with legislators, judges, and many ordinary citizens whose lives the new technology will affect. That conversation takes place through meetings, symposia, and discussions, through journal articles and media reports, through administrative and legislative hearings, and through court cases. Lawyers participate in this discussion, translating specialized knowledge into ordinary English, defining issues, often creating consensus. Typically administrators and legislators make decisions only after the conversation is well under way. Courts participate later in the process, determining whether, say, the legal result reached through this "bubbling up" is consistent with basic constitutional norms. This conversation is the "tumult," the "clamor... raised on all sides" that, Tocqueville said, "you find yourself in the midst of" when "you descend... on the soil of America." It is the democratic process in action.[3]

The nature of the law-revision problem together with the process of democratic resolution counsels a special degree of judicial modesty and caution. That is because a premature judicial decision risks short-circuiting, or preempting, the "conversational" lawmaking process—a process that embodies our modern understanding of constitutional democracy.

A recent case will illustrate the point. The Court considered a private cell phone conversation that an unknown private individual had intercepted with a scanner and delivered to a radio station. A statute forbade the broadcast of that conversation, even though the radio station itself had not planned or participated in the intercept. The case required the Court to determine the scope of the station's First Amendment right to broadcast, given the privacy interests that the statute sought to protect.[4]

Justice Stevens, speaking for four members of the Court, wrote that the key constitutional value at issue was a First Amendment interest in furthering public discussion of matters of public concern. The First Amendment trumped the statute, permitting the station to broadcast the information. But the opinion nonetheless favored a narrow holding. It focused upon the particular circumstances present in the case—the fact, for example, that the station had had nothing at all to do with obtaining the intercept. Justice O'Connor and I concurred, emphasizing the potential importance of, and the current uncertainty about, the privacy interests at issue. We explicitly left open the possibility that a broadcaster would be liable in less innocent circumstances or when less pressing public concerns favored disclosure.[5]

The narrowness of the holding itself serves a constitutional purpose. The democratic "conversation" about privacy is ongoing. In those circumstances, a Court decision that mentions its concerns without creating a binding rule could lead Congress to rewrite eavesdropping statutes, tailoring them to take account of current technological facts, such as the widespread availability of scanners and the possibility of protecting conversations through encryption. A broader constitutional rule might itself limit legislative options in ways now unforeseeable. And a broad decision is particularly dangerous when *statutory* protection of an important personal liberty is at issue. By way of contrast, the Court also recently held unconstitutional police efforts to use, without a warrant, a thermal-imaging device placed on a public sidewalk in order to identify activities within a private home. The case is different because it required the Court simply to ask whether the residents had a reasonable expectation that their activities within the house would not be disclosed to the public in this way, i.e., the privacy harm at issue is relatively clear and the applicable Fourth Amendment principle, comparatively speaking, is well established. The case required the Court not to look for new legal categories but rather to fit new technology into old categories. It was less likely that doing so would interfere with any ongoing democratic policy debate.[6]

The privacy example suggests more, in respect to judicial caution. It warns against adopting an overly rigid method of interpreting the Constitution—placing weight upon eighteenth-century details to the point at which it becomes difficult for a twenty-first-century court to apply the document's underlying values. At a minimum it suggests that courts, in determining the breadth of a constitutional holding, should look to the effect of a holding of a certain breadth on the ongoing policy-creating process. They should distinguish for those purposes between, say, the "eavesdropping" and the "thermal-imaging" kinds of cases.

The example also makes clear that it is misleading to contrast "practical" and "legal" judicial concerns. In exercising caution, a judge is not deserting the judicial role of law interpreter in order to be practical. Rather, the judge is following the law, interpreting the Constitution in light of its own practical concern for an active liberty that is itself a practical process. That is to say, the Constitution authorizes courts to proceed "practically" when they examine new laws in light of the Constitution's enduring values.

CHAPTER FIVE
AFFIRMATIVE ACTION

My first three examples have focused upon problems of participating in government, at local or federal levels, and upon problems of free speech and privacy—areas that one might describe as active liberty's natural home. My fourth example looks further afield. It focuses upon judicial efforts to determine whether a law school's affirmative action program was consistent with the Equal Protection Clause. It illustrates how reference to democratic self-government can help a court decide a different kind of constitutional question.

In the 2003 affirmative action case *Grutter v. Bollinger,* the Court considered the University of Michigan's use of race as a law school admissions criterion. The law school, an elite institution, receives about 3,500 applications each year for admission to a class of about 350. The school said that it seeks "students who individually and collectively are among the most capable," who have "substantial promise for success" in and after law school, and who will likely contribute "to the well-being of others." To obtain those students, the school considered an applicant's grade point average, Law

School Admissions Test score, and recommendations. After ruling out any applicant who it believed would not "do well enough to graduate" without "serious academic problems," it factored into its decision certain "soft variables," including the quality of the applicant's essay, the difficulty of undergraduate courses taken, unusual life experiences, and—most important for present purposes—minority race.[1]

The school sought to enroll a "critical mass" of minority students, i.e., a number sufficient to encourage "underrepresented minority students to participate in the classroom and not feel isolated." Why? The school said that it considered race as an admissions factor in order to achieve racial "diversity." It wanted diversity in order "to enrich everyone's education." And to achieve diversity it needed affirmative action, favoring groups "historically discriminated against, like African Americans, Hispanics and Native Americans." Without affirmative action, it added, those groups would not be represented in the law school student body "in meaningful numbers."[2]

The question before the Court was whether this use of race as an admissions factor by a state school was consistent with the Equal Protection Clause—a clause that forbids any state to "deny to any person ... the equal protection of the laws." The answer depended in significant part upon which of two possible interpretations of the clause the Court would accept.[3]

On the first view, the clause insists that state activity must be "color-blind." Justice Clarence Thomas, writing in dissent, explained that view as follows:

> The Constitution abhors classifications based on race, not only because those classifications can harm favored races or are based on illegitimate motives, but also because every time the government places citizens on racial registers and makes race relevant to the provision of burdens or benefits, it demeans us all. "Purchased at the price of immeasurable human suffering, the equal protection principle reflects our Nation's understanding that such classifications ultimately have a destructive impact on the individual and our society." [4]

On the second view, courts must understand the clause as more narrowly purposive. It grows out of a history that includes this nation's efforts to end slavery and the segregated society that followed. It reflects that history. It consequently demands laws that equally respect each individual; it forbids laws based on race when those laws reflect a lack of equivalent respect for members of the disfavored race; but it does not similarly disfavor race-based laws in other circumstances. Justice Ruth Bader Ginsburg, writing in a companion case, explained that view as follows:

> In implementing [the Constitution's] equality instruction...government decision makers may properly

distinguish between policies of exclusion and inclusion.... Actions designed to burden groups long denied
full citizenship stature are not sensibly ranked with
measures taken to hasten the day when entrenched discrimination and its after effects have been extirpated.[5]

The Civil War amendments sought to permit and to
encourage those "long denied full citizenship stature"
to participate fully and with equal rights in the democratic political community. Experience suggested that a
"color-blind" interpretation of those amendments, while
producing a form of equal opportunity, was insufficient
to bring about that result. Hence, in purposive terms,
invidious discrimination and positive discrimination
were not equivalent.

These two views, one color-blind, one purposive, are
not polar opposites but rather reflect different interpretive tendencies. Those who favor the "color-blind" view
nonetheless concede that *sometimes,* on rare occasions,
the clause permits distinctions based on race. Those who
favor the "narrowly purposive" view concede that courts
nonetheless must carefully scrutinize any legal classifi-
cation based on race, for without careful examination,
courts may fail to "ferret out classifications [that] in reality
[are] malign, but [that are] masquerading as benign." The
courts must also take a hard look to ensure that benign
racial preferences are "not so large as to trammel unduly
upon the opportunities of others or interfere too harshly

with legitimate expectations of persons in once-preferred groups."[6]

The Court majority in *Grutter* ultimately adopted a form of the second view. It scrutinized the law school's use of race carefully, indeed it said "strict[ly]." But it nonetheless found Michigan's diversity rationale "compelling." Because the school considered each application individually, it believed that the school's affirmative action program was "narrowly tailored" to achieve that objective. It added that it "expect[ed] that 25 years from now" this "use of racial preferences will no longer be necessary."[7]

I concentrate here on only one part of the Court's argument, namely why the Court accepted an interpretation of the Equal Protection Clause that was closer to the second than to the first view that I have advanced. The grounds for accepting that interpretation might have involved the claim that past discrimination against minorities can justify special efforts to help members of minority groups today. This claim rests upon considerations of *equality*. And equality, of course, is the underlying objective of the Equal Protection Clause. Judge John Minor Wisdom explained the claim many years ago when he said that the "Constitution is color conscious to prevent discrimination being perpetuated and to undo the effects of past discrimination." The law school's admissions policy similarly referred to the university's commitment to "diversity with special reference to the inclusion of students from groups which have been historically discriminated against." But the law school did not press this kind of equality-based remedial claim strongly. Its hesitancy may have reflected the fact that the Court in earlier cases cast doubt on the constitutional validity of affirmative action that seeks simply to remedy prior "general societal discrimination." [8]

The grounds for accepting the "narrowly purposive" view might have included a *liberty*-based claim—a claim that the Constitution grants universities especially broad authority to determine for themselves the composition of their student bodies. Justice Lewis Powell, for example, wrote in *Regents of the University of California v. Bakke* that the "freedom of a university to make its own judgements as to education includes the selection of its student body." The Michigan law school argued for a more fully participatory form of education, stating that "in the context of higher education," a compelling state interest includes a "diversity" that promises "educational benefits," "help[ing to] break down racial stereotypes," enabling "students to better understand persons of different races," "promot[ing] cross-racial understanding," and producing "livelier, more spirited, and simply more enlightening and interesting" discussions. The Court, accepting a form of this argument, pointed out that "given the important purpose of public education and the expansive freedoms of speech and thought associated with the university environment, universities occupy a special niche in our constitutional tradition." But the Court's opinion does not suggest that these considerations, related to free expression, are determinative.[9]

Instead, the Court placed important weight upon certain practical considerations, which Justice O'Connor, writing for the Court, described as follows:

> [M]ajor American businesses have made clear that the skills needed in today's increasingly global marketplace can only be developed through exposure to widely diverse people, cultures, ideas, and viewpoints.[10]

She added:

> [H]igh-ranking retired officers and civilian leaders of the United States military assert that "based on [their] decades of experience," a "highly qualified, racially diverse officer corps... is essential to the military's ability to fulfill its principal mission to provide national security." [11]

She then said:

> Student body diversity... better prepares students for an increasingly diverse workforce and society, and better prepares them as professionals.... [E]ducation [is] pivotal to sustaining our political and cultural heritage

[and plays] a fundamental role in maintaining the fabric of society.[12]

She drew these considerations together with these words:

[N]owhere is the importance of... openness more acute than in the context of higher education. Effective participation by members of all racial and ethnic groups in the civic life of our Nation is essential if the dream of one Nation, indivisible, is to be realized.... [Indeed,] the path to leadership [must] be *visibly* open to talented and qualified individuals of every race and ethnicity. All members of our heterogeneous society must have confidence in the openness and integrity of the educational institutions that provide this training.... [And] all [must] participate.[13]

What are these arguments but an appeal to principles of solidarity, to principles of *fraternity,* to principles of *active liberty?* They find some form of affirmative action necessary to maintain a well-functioning participatory democracy. They say that an interpretation of the Equal Protection Clause that would outlaw the law school's affirmative action program is an interpretation that, from the perspective of the Constitution's basic democratic objectives, would not work. Too many individuals of all races would lack experience with a racially diverse educational environment helpful for their later effective participation in today's diverse civil society. Too many individuals of minority race would find the doors of higher education closed; those closed doors would shut them out of positions of leadership in the armed forces, in business, and in government as well; and too many would conclude that the nation and its governmental processes are *theirs*, not *ours*. If these are the likely consequences—as many knowledgeable groups told the Court they were—could our democratic form of government then function as the Framers intended?

When faced with one interpretation of the Equal Protection Clause that, through efforts to include, would facilitate the functioning of democracy and a different interpretation of the Equal Protection Clause that, through perceived exclusion, might impede the functioning of that democracy, is it surprising that the Court majority chose the former? Is that interpretation not more compatible with a Constitution that seeks to create a democratic government able, as a practical matter, to function? Given that constitutional objective, it is not surprising that the Court interpreted the Equal Protection Clause in a way that diminishes the risk of serious racial division—a division that exclusion from elite educational institutions would aggravate. Nor should it be completely surprising that, in light of similar risks created through excessive racial self-identification and resulting strife, the majority wrote of its "expectation" that in twenty-five years policies like the law school's would no longer be necessary.[14]

Sometimes reference to active liberty can help a court choose between competing interpretations of constitutional provisions that, on their face, seem based upon other values. *Grutter* shows how this is so.

CHAPTER SIX

STATUTORY INTERPRETATION

The fifth example concerns statutory interpretation. It contrasts a literal text-based approach with an approach that places more emphasis on statutory purpose and congressional intent. It illustrates why judges should pay primary attention to a statute's purpose in difficult cases of interpretation in which language is not clear. It shows how overemphasis on text can lead courts astray, divorcing law from life— indeed, creating law that harms those whom Congress meant to help. And it explains why a purposive approach is more consistent with the framework for a "delegated democracy" that the Constitution creates.[1]

The interpretive problem arises when statutory language does not clearly answer the question of what the statute means or how it applies. Why does a statute contain such language? Perhaps Congress used inappropriate language. Perhaps it failed to use its own drafting expertise or failed to have committee hearings, writing legislation on the floor instead. Perhaps it chose politically symbolic language or ambiguous language over more precise language—possibilities that modern, highly partisan, interest-group-based politics (responding to overly simplified media accounts) make realistic. Perhaps no one in Congress thought about how the statute would apply in certain circumstances. Perhaps it is impossible to use language that foresees how a statute should apply in all relevant circumstances.

The founding generation of Americans understood these or similar possibilities. They realized that judges, though mere "fallible men," would have to exercise judgement and discretion in applying newly codified law. But they expected that judges, when doing so, would remain faithful to the legislators' will. The problem of statutory interpretation is how to meet that expectation.

Most judges start in the same way. They look first to the statute's language, its structure, and its history in an effort to determine the statute's purpose. They then use that purpose (along with the language, structure, and history) to determine the proper interpretation. Thus far, there is agreement. But when the problem is truly difficult, these factors without more may simply limit the universe of possible answers without clearly identifying a final choice. What then?

At this point judges tend to divide in their approach. Some look primarily to text, i.e., to language and text-related circumstances, for further enlightenment. They may try to tease further meaning from the language and structure of the statute itself. They may look to language-based canons of interpretation in the search for an "objective" key to the statute's proper interpretation, say a canon like *noscitur a sociis,* which tells a judge to interpret a word so that it has the same kind of meaning as its neighbors. Textualism, it has been argued, searches for "meaning...in structure." It means "preferring the language and structure of the law whenever possible over its legislative history and imputed values." It asks judges to avoid invocation of vague or broad statutory purposes and instead to consider such purposes at "lower levels of generality." It hopes thereby to reduce the risk that judges will interpret statutes subjectively, substituting their own ideas of what is good for those of Congress.[2]

Other judges look primarily to the statute's purposes for enlightenment. They avoid the use of interpretive canons. They allow context to determine the level of generality at which they will describe a statute's purpose—in the way that context tells us not to answer the lost driver's request for directions, "Where am I?" with the words "In a car." They speak in terms of congressional "intent," while understanding that legal conventions govern the use of that term to describe, not the intent of any, or every, individual legislator, but the intent of the group— in the way that linguistic conventions allow us to speak of the intentions of an army or a team, even when they differ from those of any, or every, soldier or member. And they examine legislative history, often closely, in the hope that the history will help them better understand the context, the enacting legislators' objectives, and ultimately the statute's purposes. At the heart of a purpose-based approach stands the "reasonable member of Congress"—a legal fiction that applies, for example, even when Congress did not in fact consider a particular problem. The judge will ask how this person (real or fictional), aware of the statute's language, structure, and general objectives (actually or hypothetically), *would have wanted* a court to interpret the statute in light of present circumstances in the particular case.

Three recent cases illustrate the difference between the two approaches. In each the majority followed a more textual approach; the dissent, a more purposive approach.

Case One

The Foreign Sovereign Immunities Act says that a foreign nation, when it is a defendant in commercial litigation, can sometimes successfully assert a defense of "sovereign immunity" and thereby avoid liability. When the applicability of the act (including its many exceptions to the sovereign immunity rule) is in doubt—say because the plaintiff claims that a defendant corporation, even if part of a foreign government, is an ordinary commercial enterprise—the defendant can remove the case to federal court to permit a federal judge to decide whether or how the act should apply. But a defendant can do so only if "a majority of" its "shares or other ownership interest is owned by" a foreign nation.[3]

An illustration of the issue in the case might go as follows: Suppose that Ruritania's government owns 100 per cent of Ruritania Furniture Company's stock. If a plaintiff sues the company in a state court, Ruritania Furniture can remove the case to federal court to permit the federal judge to determine how the act applies. But suppose the state court plaintiff sues not Ruritania Furniture Company but Ruritania Chair Company, a subsidiary of Ruritania Furniture. Suppose further that Ruritania Furniture owns 100 per cent of the stock of Ruritania Chair. If Ruritania owns Ruritania Furniture, which in turn owns Ruritania Chair, can Ruritania Chair remove the case to federal court? Does it qualify under the statute? Does Ruritania's ownership of a parent that in turn owns a subsidiary mean, in the words of the statute, that Ruritania possesses an "other ownership interest" in the subsidiary? If so, Ruritania Chair can remove the case; otherwise it cannot.[4]

Judges using a more literal text-based approach are likely to find that the wholly owned subsidiary of the wholly owned parent cannot remove the case. The majority of my Court reasoned: American corporate law ordinarily considers a corporation and its shareholders as distinct entities. Thus, ordinarily the law deems that the corporation, not the government that owns the corporation, is the owner of the corporate subsidiary. Other linguistic clues reinforce this point. For example, had Congress wished to depart from this ordinary rule, it might have used the phrase "direct *and indirect* ownership." That phrase, found in some other statutes, would have signaled a congressional intent to disregard the ordinary corporate "structural ownership rule." But Congress did not use it. Instead, Congress wrote language that refers both to (1) "other ownership interest" and also (2) "ownership of a majority of... shares." To give strong meaning to the word "other," we should interpret it to mean "other than ownership of stock." And the need to read the word "other" in this way is supported by the interpretive canon that says that "a statute must, if possible, be construed in such fashion that every word has some operative effect." These linguistic and structural facts, taken together, indicate that the words "other ownership interest" do not include ownership of shares in a parent that, in turn, owns a subsidiary.[5]

A more purpose-oriented judge will likely come to the opposite conclusion. The dissenters in the same case reasoned: The purpose of the act's jurisdictional provision is to bring into federal court cases in which a foreign government owns a commercial defendant. The act will thereby allow the foreign government to take advantage of federal procedural protections that state court systems sometimes lack. Given this purpose, why would Congress, or any reasonable member of Congress, want to grant this "protection to a Foreign Nation acting through a Corporate Parent but deny the same protection to the Foreign Nation acting through, for example, a wholly owned Corporate Subsidiary?" There is no good answer to this question. At the same time, the dissenters said, a more literal textual interpretation would unnecessarily complicate the business of corporate structuring. It would tell those engaged in that work that they must consider a new nonbusiness-related factor—a legal jurisdictional factor—when they decide whether to structure a government business with one, or with two or more, tiers. There is no reason to do so. The dissenters recognize that the statute's language must permit their purpose-based interpretation. They pointed to Justice Holmes's comment in a similar case: The purpose-based interpretation does not "ignore the distinction between a corporation and its members." It simply interprets an untechnical word "ownership" in the liberal way that Congress intended.[6]

Case Two

The Federal Arbitration Act, written to overcome judicial hostility to arbitration, says that all courts, including state courts, must enforce arbitration clauses written into contracts—indeed, written into any contract that the Commerce Clause gives Congress the power to control. The act makes an exception for arbitration clauses contained in "contracts of employment of seamen, railroad employees, *or any other class of workers engaged in foreign or interstate commerce.*" A retail store and one of its employees enter into an ordinary employment contract that contains an arbitration clause. The Arbitration Act applies—and state courts must enforce the clause—unless the employment contract falls within the exception. And it does so only if retail store employees fall within the term "any other class of workers."

A Court majority, following a more literal, text-based approach, concluded that the words "any other class of workers" did not include those who work in retail stores. The relevant words, it pointed out, follow an explicit reference to "seamen" and to "railroad employees." A canon of statutory interpretation, *ejusdem generis*, says that, if "general words follow specific words in a statutory enumeration," courts should construe the "general words" as "embrac[ing] only objects similar in nature to those objects enumerated by the preceding specific words." And retail store workers are not similar in nature to seamen and railway workers.[7]

The majority drew support from other words in the relevant phrase, the words "in commerce." Those words have become a term of art, signaling that Congress intends a limited, rather than a full, exercise of its Commerce Clause power. The majority added that its interpretation, which limits "other class of workers" to, say, transportation workers, is consistent with a *limited* exercise of Congress's commerce power, but an interpretation broad enough to include workers in retail stores is too broad to count as limited. The majority recognized that the words "in commerce" had not become words of art in 1923 when

Congress enacted the statute. But it thought that reading those words more broadly in older statutes would "bring instability" to the interpretive task.[8]

The dissent believed that the words "any other class of workers" referred to all workers, retail store employees included. Taking a more directly purposive approach, it began by asking why Congress included the exception at all. The act's legislative history—embodied in testimony before the relevant Senate committee—made clear that the seamen's union had opposed the Arbitration Act's enactment because it feared that arbitration in respect to employment would disfavor ordinary workers. Seeking to overcome this opposition, the American Bar Association, the statute's chief proponent (and drafter of its language), testified that it wanted to help bring about arbitration of commercial disputes, not of employment disputes. It said that it had no interest in affecting "labor disputes." The testifying ABA official added, "if your honorable committee should feel that there is any danger of that, they should add to the bill the following language, 'but nothing herein contained shall apply to seamen or any class of workers in interstate and foreign commerce.'" Herbert Hoover, then Secretary of Commerce, seconded the thought in his own testimony.[9]

If this testimony adequately describes the exception's purpose—and nothing in the history suggests any contrary purpose—Congress would have wanted the exception to cover all workers. To the extent that it did not, Congress's objective would be compromised. The words "in commerce" do not show the contrary, for that phrase was not a term of art in 1923 when Congress wrote the act. Nor does the fact that the exception lists "seamen" and "railroad employees." After all, in 1923 Court decisions had led Congress to believe that its commerce powers were limited—perhaps in this area primarily to workers like those in transportation who helped to move goods from state to state. Congress might have wanted its language to emphasize that it had exempted the groups of workers then most directly affected, particularly since, by doing so, it could assure those opposed to the law, seamen, that they had nothing to fear. Over time courts have read the Commerce Clause more broadly, and, since the act's language ties its scope to the clause, they have thereby extended the reach of the act itself. Why would Congress not have wanted an expanding exception of similar scope?[10]

Does it matter that the textualist view of the statute prevailed? As a result states cannot disfavor arbitration clauses in most employment contracts. Some would argue that this result is good. Labor arbitration has worked well in areas subject to labor board regulation— in which labor disputes are typically subject to arbitration for other legal reasons. Others might argue the contrary. But if one sees the interpretive process as an effort to locate, and remain faithful to, the human purposes embodied in a statute, how can one admire this result?

The only direct evidence available—I would say the *only* evidence available—indicates that, at the time of the statute's enactment, members of Congress saw a problem—a problem involving arbitration of commercial contracts. They tried to attack that problem with a statute tailored to the problem's scope—deliberately eliminating labor contracts from the statute's coverage. Yet the Court has responded by extending the statute's scope so that it now regulates an area of life that members of Congress would originally have thought excluded, which exclusion they desired and sought.

Case Three

The federal habeas corpus statute is ambiguous in respect to the time limits that apply when a state prisoner seeks access to federal habeas corpus. It says that a state prisoner (ordinarily) must file a federal petition within one year after his state court conviction becomes final. But the statute tolls that one-year period during the time that "a properly filed application for State post-conviction *or other collateral review*" is pending. Do the words "other collateral review" include an earlier application for a federal habeas corpus petition? Should the one-year period be tolled, for example, when a state prisoner mistakenly files a habeas petition in federal court before he exhausts all his state collateral remedies?[11]

It is unlikely that anyone in Congress thought about this question, for it is highly technical. Yet it is important. More than half of all federal habeas corpus petitions fall into the relevant category—i.e., state prisoners file them prematurely before the prisoner has tried to take advantage of available state remedies. In those cases, the federal court often dismisses the petition and the state prisoner must return to state court to exhaust available state remedies before he can once again file his federal habeas petition in federal court. If the one-year statute of limitations is not tolled while the first federal habeas petition was pending, that state prisoner will likely find that the one year has run— and his federal petition is time-barred— before he can return to federal court.[12]

A literal reading of the statute suggests that this is just what Congress had in mind. It suggests that the one-year time limit is tolled only during the time that *state* collateral review (or similar) proceedings are in process. And that reading is supported by various linguistic canons of construction.[13]

Nonetheless, the language does not foreclose an alternative interpretation—an interpretation under which such petitions would fall within the scope of the phrase "other collateral review." The word "State" could be read to modify the phrase "post-conviction . . . review," permitting "*other* collateral review" to refer to federal proceedings. The phrase "properly filed" could be interpreted to refer to purely formal filing requirements rather than calling into play more important remedial questions such as the presence or absence of "exhaustion." A purposive approach favors this latter linguistic interpretation.[14]

Why? Refer back to our hypothetical legislator, the reasonable member of Congress. Which interpretation would that member favor (if he had thought of the problem, which he likely had not)? Consider the consequences of the more literal interpretation. That interpretation would close the doors of federal habeas courts to many or most state prisoners who mistakenly filed a federal habeas petition too soon, but not to all such prisoners. Whether the one-year window was still open would depend in large part on how long the federal court considering the premature federal petition took to dismiss it. In cases in which the court ruled quickly, the short time the federal petition was (wrongly) present in the federal court might not matter. But if a premature federal petition languishes on the federal court's docket while the one year runs, the petitioner would likely lose his one meaningful chance to seek federal habeas relief. By way of contrast, state court delay in considering a prisoner petition in state court would not matter. Whenever *state* proceedings are at issue, the statute tolls the one-year limitations period.

Now ask *why* our reasonable legislator would want to bring about these consequences. He might believe that state prisoners have too often abused the federal writ by filing too many petitions. But the distinction that a literal interpretation would make between those allowed to file and those not allowed to file—a distinction that in essence rests upon federal court processing delay—is a *random* distinction, bearing no logical relation to any abuse-related purpose. Would our reasonable legislator, even if concerned about abuse of the writ, choose to deny access to the Great Writ on a *random* basis? Given our traditions, including those the Constitution grants through its habeas corpus guarantees, the answer to this question is likely no. Would those using a more literal text-based approach answer this question differently? I do not think so. But my real objection to the text-based approach is that it would prevent them from posing the question at all.[15]

I mean my three examples to suggest the danger that lurks where judges rely too heavily upon just text and textual aids when interpreting a statute. I mean them to indicate why, when difficult statutory questions are at issue, courts do better to focus foremost upon statutory purpose, ruling out neither legislative history nor any other form of help in order to locate the role that Congress intended the statutory words in question to play.

For one thing, near-exclusive reliance upon canons and other linguistic interpretive aids in close cases can undermine the Constitution's democratic objective. Legislation in a delegated democracy is meant to embody the people's will, either directly (in so far as legislators see themselves as translating how their constituents feel about each proposed law) or indirectly (in so far as

legislators see themselves as exercising delegated authority to vote in accordance with what they see as the public
interest). Either way, an interpretation of a statute that
tends to implement the legislator's will helps to implement the public's will and is therefore consistent with the
Constitution's democratic purpose. For similar reasons
an interpretation that undercuts the statute's objectives
tends to undercut that constitutional objective.

I concede that: were the courts fully consistent in
their use of the canons; were congressional drafters fully
aware of those canons; were Congress to rely consistently upon the work of those drafters; in a word, were the
same linguistic conventions known and used similarly
by all; then reliance upon those conventions alone could
provide interpretations likely to reflect congressional
purposes. But in the world as it is, we shall do better to
use whatever tools best identify congressional purpose in
the circumstances.

Use of a "reasonable legislator" fiction also facilitates
legislative accountability. Ordinary citizens think in
terms of general purposes. They readily understand their
elected legislators' thinking similarly. It is not impossible to ask an ordinary citizen to determine whether a
particular law is consistent with a general purpose the
ordinary citizen might support. It is not impossible to ask
an ordinary citizen to determine what general purpose a
legislator sought to achieve in enacting a particular statute. And it is not impossible for the ordinary citizen to

judge the legislator accordingly. But it *is* impossible to ask an ordinary citizen (or an ordinary legislator) to understand the operation of linguistic canons of interpretation. And it *is* impossible to ask an ordinary citizen to draw any relevant electoral conclusion from consequences that might flow when courts reach a purpose-thwarting interpretation of the statute based upon their near-exclusive use of interpretive canons. Were a segment of the public unhappy about application of the Arbitration Act to ordinary employment contracts, whom should it blame?

For another thing, that approach means that laws will work better for the people they are presently meant to affect. Law is tied to life, and a failure to understand how a statute is so tied can undermine the very human activity that the law seeks to benefit. The more literal text-based, canon-based interpretation of the Foreign Sovereign Immunities jurisdictional statute, for example, means that foreign nations, those using tiered corporate ownership, will find their access to federal courts cut off, undermining the statute's basic jurisdictional objectives. The textual approach to the habeas corpus statute randomly closes courthouse doors in a way that runs contrary to our commitment to basic individual liberty. And it does so because it tends to stop judges from asking a relevant purpose-based question: Why would Congress have wanted a statute that produces those consequences?[16]

In sum, a "reasonable legislator" approach is a workable method of implementing the Constitution's democratic objective. It permits ready translation of the general desire of the public for certain ends, through the legislator's efforts to embody those ends in legislation, into a set of statutory words that will carry out those general objectives. I have argued that the Framers created the Constitution's complex governmental mechanism in order better to translate public will, determined through collective deliberation, into sound public policy. The courts constitute part of that mechanism. And judicial use of the "will of the reasonable legislator"—even if at times it is a fiction—helps statutes match their means to their overall public policy objectives, a match that helps translate the popular will into sound policy. An overly literal reading of a text can too often stand in the way.

CHAPTER SEVEN

ADMINISTRATIVE LAW

The final example returns to a question common to all modern democracies, one that I discussed earlier in the context of federalism. How can we reconcile democratic control of government with the technical nature of modern life? The former calls for decision-making by citizens or their elected representatives, the latter for decision-making by administrators or experts. If we delegate too much decision-making authority to experts, administration and democracy conflict. We lose control. Yet if we delegate too little authority, we also find democracy weakened. To achieve our democratically chosen ends in a modern populous society requires some amount of administration, involving administrative, not democratic, decision-making. To achieve those same ends in a technologically advanced society requires expertise. The average citizen normally lacks the time, knowledge, and experience necessary to understand certain technical matters related, for example, to the environment, energy, communications, or modern weaponry. Without delegation to experts, an inexpert public, possessing the will, would lack the way. The public understand this fact.

Who would want to vote about how an army battalion should take the next hill? The Framers foresaw this possibility. They sought to create a workable democracy—a democratic process capable of acting for the public good.

To reconcile democratically chosen ends with administrative expertise requires striking a balance—some delegation, but not too much. The right balance avoids conflict between democracy and administration. The latter then complements the former by implementing legislatively determined general policy objectives. How to strike that balance? That is the mystery. The Constitution, not surprisingly, leaves the matter primarily in the hands of the legislature. Its legislative handiwork, the statute, is subject to court interpretation on this point as on others. And that is where administrative law plays a role. As classically conceived, administrative law helps to implement the legislature's choice of when and how to delegate decision-making to administrators and experts.

This final example focuses upon a related principle of administrative law, a principle of judicial "deference" to agency interpretation of statutes. The principle applies when judges and administrative agencies seek to interpret the same statutory provision. Should a judge give weight to the agency's interpretation of its governing statute, perhaps deferring to the agency, substituting its view of the statute for the judge's own? If so, when? And why? In *Chevron USA v. Natural Resources Defense Council, Inc.,* the Court held that a judge should defer to a reasonable agency interpretation of an ambiguous statute. It said that the "power of an administrative agency to administer a congressionally created...program necessarily requires the formulation of policy and the making of rules to fill any gap left, implicitly or explicitly, by Congress." And "a court may not substitute its own construction of a statutory provision for a reasonable interpretation made by the administrator of an agency." As one of my colleagues has written, *Chevron* seems to require deference to "an authoritative [and reasonable] agency position," unless "(1) the statute is unambiguous, so there is no room for administrative interpretation; (2) no interpretation has been made by personnel of the agency responsible for administering the statute; or (3) the [reasonable] interpretation made by such personnel was not authoritative, in the sense that it does not represent the official position of the expert agency."[1]

Suppose, for example, that a labor relations statute requires a federal agency to "meet" with its employees' collective bargaining representative and "negotiate in good faith for the purposes of arriving at a collective bargaining agreement." These words do not say *when* that good-faith negotiation must take place. They do not say whether the agency must renegotiate if an important new matter comes up, say, in the third year of a five-year contract. The statutory language is ambiguous. And the answers yes, no, or it depends (say, on what the parties agreed to about reopening in midstream) all seem reasonable. Hence, given *Chevron,* a judge should defer to the agency's own statutory answer. The agency, not the court, will thereby determine the meaning of the statute.[2]

Judges do not agree about how absolute *Chevron's* approach is meant to be. Is it a judicially created absolute rule? Is it just a rule of thumb? How shall we interpret that rule of interpretation? To refer back to the democratic origins and purposes of delegation itself will help answer this question.

What lies behind *Chevron?* What is its rationale? The answers in part seem practical. No one can foresee all possible applications of a statute. Legislation inevitably contains ambiguities and gaps. The agency that administers the statute is likely better able than a court to know how best to fill those gaps. The agency, experienced in administering the statute, will likely better understand the practical implications of competing alternative interpretations, consistency with congressional objectives, administrative difficulties, the consequences for the public and so forth.

But the answer is not entirely practical. Principles of active liberty also matter. Looked at from a democratic perspective, *Chevron* helps a judge answer an important question about Congress: how, in this statute, did Congress strike the democratic/administrative balance? Did Congress intend for the courts to defer to the agency's own interpretive views or did Congress intend *not* to delegate the interpretive decision to the agency (thereby asking the courts to treat the statute like any other)? It is quite possible that no member of Congress actually thought about the matter. But a judge still can ask how a reasonable member of Congress would have answered it had the question come to mind. The judge can ask whether, given the statutory aims and circumstances, a hypothetical member would likely have wanted judicial deference in this situation.

Does framing the question as referring to a member of Congress matter? Will it not normally lead to the same answer that practical considerations alone would suggest? After all, a reasonable member of Congress would want the statute to work well; that member would know that interpretation plays an important role in assuring that result; and that member would realize that in most instances judges possess less relevant expertise than does the administering agency. Hence that member would likely conclude, as did the Court in *Chevron,* that ordinarily judges should listen carefully to the agency's views about proper interpretation. If the statute is ambiguous, courts should defer to a reasonable agency interpretation of a statute. So if the deference-related result is the same, why bother imagining a hypothetical member of Congress?

Active liberty, however, suggests that it does matter. Indeed, it suggests that *Chevron*'s rule is not absolute but simply a rule of thumb. Deference to a reasonable agency interpretation of an ambiguous statutory provision often makes sense, but not always. Suppose, for example, a statutory ambiguity arises in the context of a question of national importance. Does a "foreman" count as an "employee" under Section 2 of the National Labor Relations Act, thereby falling within the act's protections? Does the statute forbidding discrimination in employment based upon "age" forbid discrimination against younger workers, as well as against older workers? Would our hypothetical reasonable member of Congress have wanted a regulatory agency to decide such questions of major importance? Whenever a statutory term, though ambiguous, concerns a matter that Congress is likely to have wanted to decide for itself, our construct—the reasonable member—leads us to conclude that courts should *not* defer. And that is how our Court has treated most such questions.[3]

To take another example, suppose that the agency has expressed its views in an informal manner—a manual of internal procedures, a press release, or a letter written by low-level officials. Should that agency viewpoint nonetheless carry weight in the interpretive enterprise? The "reasonable member of Congress" approach will lead the courts to ask whether it makes sense to defer to a particular kind of agency interpretation given the particular kind of statute and the particular circumstances at issue. The answer will be, sometimes yes, sometimes no—more or less what our cases have held.[4]

Treating *Chevron* in this way—not as an absolute rule, but as a rule of thumb—may seem to complicate life for agencies, lawyers, and judges. But particular circumstances can generate clear (if narrow and specific) legal answers; and those answers may make more sense than answers that would flow from a more absolute, overarching interpretive rule. As important, those answers make *democratic* sense. In all likelihood a hypothetical reasonable member of Congress *would have* decided the delegation/deference question so as to help the statute work better to achieve its ends. And those ends usually reflect the general desires of the public. Use of the fiction thereby helps the statute work better, in both the functional and the democratic sense of the term. And, in doing so, it makes it easier for the public to hold accountable for the results both Congress and those whom Congress has charged with the task of implementing the statute.

The practical need and the theoretical democratic reasons for using the "reasonable legislator" merge. The fiction helps to make the law reflect the public's desire for a law that implements its general instructions. Active liberty provides a democratic rationale for better functioning administrative law.

CHAPTER EIGHT

PURPOSIVE INTERPRETATION

My six examples have focused on different areas of the law—free speech, federalism, privacy, affirmative action, statutory interpretation, and judicial review of administrative action. The discussion of each involved contemporary problems of modern government—campaign finance, environmental regulation, technology-based privacy risks, affirmative action, the legislative and administrative processes. I have tried to show how, in varying contexts, reference to the Constitution's basic democratic objectives can help courts shape constitutional doctrine, reconcile competing constitutional values, time judicial intervention, interpret statutory ambiguities, and create room for agency interpretations. The discussion has suggested that I, a judge who has a role in playing the complex score provided me in the form of constitutional and statutory text, history, structure, and precedent, can perform my role with less discord, more faithfully to the entire enterprise, and with stronger justification for the power I wield in a government that is of, by, and for the people, by paying close attention to the Constitution's democratic active liberty objective.

By now it should be clear that when I argue for greater attention, I am not arguing for a new theory of constitutional law. In my experience, most judges approach and decide most cases, including constitutional cases, quite similarly. They are professionals. And their professional training and experience leads them to examine language, history, tradition, precedent, purpose, and consequences. Given roughly similar forms of legal education and professional experience, it is not surprising that judges often agree about how these factors, taken together, point to the proper result in a particular case. Even when they differ, the degree of difference is often small. Our Court, which normally steps in where other judges disagree, decides roughly 40 per cent of its cases unanimously. Most of the rest involve only one or two dissenting votes. In only about 20 per cent of our caseload do we divide five–four. And the same Justices are not always on the same side of the split. Only a handful of constitutional and statutory issues are as open in respect to language, history, and basic purpose as those I have here described.[1]

I have taken this professional framework as a given. Within that framework, I have argued for greater awareness of, and emphasis upon, the Constitution's democratic imperative. My argument has not rested upon logical or scientifically convincing empirical demonstration. Rather it has used examples to suggest a pattern. And that pattern, in turn, suggests that supplementing ordinary, professional judicial approaches with increased emphasis on the Constitution's democratic objective will help Americans remain true to the past while better resolving their contemporary problems of government through law.

The interpretive tradition that I follow

At the same time, I recognize that the question of how a constitutional judge goes about his or her work is often controversial. Indeed, the judge's approach to constitutional interpretation can become a subject of debate, not only among lawyers and judges, but among the public at large, including politically active citizens. And it is consequently important for the public in general to understand how judges reach decisions, including decisions made about politically controversial matters.

Thus, I recognize that the methods I have used in my illustrations are themselves controversial. They reflect an interpretive tradition that I have learned and in which I work. That tradition encompasses a particular view of *democracy*, as including not only the "rights of the whole people," but also "the duties of the whole people." And it calls for *judicial restraint*, basing that call upon both technical circumstance and democratic value. As to the first, "[c]ourts are ill-equipped to make the investigations which should precede" most legislation. As to the second, a judge's "agreement or disagreement" about the wisdom of a law "has nothing to do with the right of a majority to embody their opinions in law." For both kinds of reasons, even if a judge knows "what the just result should be," that judge "is not to substitute even his juster will" for that of "the people." In a constitutional democracy "a deep-seated conviction on the part of the people...is entitled to great respect."[2]

That tradition sees texts as driven by *purposes*. The judge should try to find and "honestly...say what was the underlying purpose expressed" in a statute. The judge should read constitutional language "as the revelation of the great purposes which were intended to be achieved by the Constitution" itself, a "framework for" and a "continuing instrument of government." The judge should recognize that the Constitution will apply to "new subject matter...with which the framers were not familiar." Thus, the judge, whether applying statute or Constitution, should "reconstruct the past solution imaginatively in its setting and project the purposes which inspired it upon the concrete occasions which arise for their decision." Since law is connected to life, judges, in applying a text in light of its purpose, should look to *consequences*, including "contemporary conditions, social, industrial, and political, of the community to be affected." And since "the purpose of construction is the ascertainment of meaning, nothing that is logically relevant should be excluded."[3]

That tradition does not expect highly general instructions themselves to determine the outcome of difficult concrete cases where language is open-ended and precisely defined purpose is difficult to ascertain. Certain constitutional language, for example, reflects "fundamental aspirations and... 'moods,' embodied in provisions like the due process and equal protection clauses, which were designed not to be precise and positive directions for rules of action." A judge, when interpreting such open-ended provisions, must avoid being "willful, in the sense of enforcing individual views." A judge cannot "enforce whatever he thinks best." "In the exercise of" the "high power" of judicial review, says Justice Louis Brandeis, "we must be ever on our guard, lest we erect our prejudices into legal principles." At the same time, a judge must avoid being "wooden, in uncritically resting on formulas, in assuming the familiar to be the necessary, in not realizing that any problem can be solved if only one principle is involved but that, unfortunately, all controversies of importance involve if not a conflict at least an interplay of principles." [4]

How, then, is the judge to act between the bounds of the "willful" and the "wooden"? The tradition answers with an *attitude,* an attitude that hesitates to rely upon any single theory or grand view of law, of interpretation, or of the Constitution. It champions the need to search for purposes; it calls for restraint, asking judges to "speak... humbly as the voice of the law." And it finds in the democratic nature of our system more than simply a justification for judicial restraint. Holmes reminds the judge as a general matter to allow "[c]onsiderable latitude... for differences of view." And Learned Hand describes both legislative and judicial democratic attitudes when he says that the "spirit which seeks to understand the minds of other men and women," the "spirit which weighs their interests alongside its own without bias," is the "spirit of liberty" itself.[5]

My discussion of active liberty falls within the broad outlines of the tradition these statements suggest. But it takes place in a different time. The statements I quote, from Justices Holmes, Brandeis, Stone, Frankfurter, and Judge Hand, must be read in light of later decisions that abolished legal segregation, that gave life to the Constitution's liberty-protecting promises, that helped to make "We the People" a phrase that finally includes those whom the Constitution originally and intentionally ignored. The discussion welcomes those decisions as furthering the Constitution's basic objectives. One of my objectives is to illustrate why one can, without philosophical contradiction, essentially embrace the later decisions without essentially abandoning the traditional attitude. That is to say, the philosophical tension is sometimes less than some have imagined.[6]

Following the tradition just described, I have urged attention to purpose and consequences. My discussion sees individual constitutional provisions as embodying certain basic purposes, often expressed in highly general terms. It sees the Constitution itself as a single document designed to further certain basic general purposes as a whole. It argues that an understanding of, and a focus upon, those general purposes will help a judge better to understand and to apply specific provisions. And it identifies consequences as an important yardstick to measure a given interpretation's faithfulness to these democratic purposes. In short, focus on purpose seeks to promote active liberty by insisting on interpretations, statutory as well as constitutional, that are consistent with the people's will. Focus on consequences, in turn, allows us to gauge whether and to what extent we have succeeded in facilitating workable outcomes which reflect that will.

A serious objection

As I said, the approach, indeed the tradition, just described is not uncontroversial. Some lawyers, judges, and scholars would caution strongly against the reliance upon purposes (particularly abstractly stated purposes) and assessment of consequences. They ask judges to focus primarily upon text, upon the Framers' original expectations, narrowly conceived, and upon historical tradition. They do not deny the occasional relevance of consequences or purposes (including such general purposes as democracy), but they believe that judges should use them sparingly in the interpretive endeavor. They ask judges who tend to find interpretive answers in those decision-making elements to rethink the problem to see whether language, history, tradition, and precedent by themselves will not yield an answer. They fear that, once judges become accustomed to justifying legal conclusions through appeal to real-world consequences, they will too often act subjectively and undemocratically, substituting an elite's views of good policy for sound law. They hope that language, history, tradition, and precedent will provide important safeguards against a judge's confusing his or her personal, undemocratic notion of what is good for that which the Constitution or statute demands. They tend also to emphasize the need for judicial opinions that set forth their legal conclusions in terms of rules that will guide other institutions, including lower courts.[7]

This view, which I shall call "textualist" (in respect to statutes) or "originalist" (in respect to the Constitution) or "literalist" (shorthand for both), while logically consistent with emphasizing the Constitution's democratic objectives, is not hospitable to the kinds of arguments I have advanced. Nor is it easily reconciled with my illustrations. Why, then, does it not undercut my entire argument?

The answer, in my view, lies in the unsatisfactory nature of that interpretive approach. First, the more "originalist" judges cannot appeal to the Framers themselves in support of their interpretive views. The Framers did not say specifically what factors judges should take into account when they interpret statutes or the Constitution. This is obvious in the case of statutes. Why would the Framers have preferred (1) a system of interpretation that relies heavily on linguistic canons to (2) a system that seeks more directly to find the intent of the legislators who enacted the statute? It is close to obvious in respect to the Constitution. Why would the Framers, who disagreed even about the necessity of *including* a Bill of Rights in the Constitution, who disagreed about the *content* of that Bill of Rights, nonetheless have agreed about *what school of interpretive thought* should prove dominant in interpreting that Bill of Rights in the centuries to come?[8]

In respect to content, the Constitution itself says that the "enumeration" in the Constitution of some rights "shall not be construed to deny or disparage others retained by the people." Professor Bailyn concludes that the Framers added this language to make clear that "rights, like law itself, should never be fixed, frozen, that new dangers and needs will emerge, and that to respond to these dangers and needs, rights must be newly specified to protect the individual's integrity and inherent dignity." Given the open-ended nature of *content,* why should one expect to find fixed views about the nature of interpretive practices?[9]

If, however, justification for the literalist's interpretive practices cannot be found in the Framers' intentions, where can it be found—other than in an appeal to *consequences,* that is, in an appeal to the presumed beneficial consequences for the law or for the nation that will flow from adopting those practices? And that is just what we find argued. That is to say, literalist arguments often try to show that that approach will have favorable *results,* for example, that it will deter judges from substituting their own views about what is good for the public for those of Congress or for those embodied in the Constitution. They argue, in other words, that a more literal approach to interpretation will better control judicial subjectivity. Thus, while literalists eschew consideration of consequences case by case, their interpretive rationale is consequentialist in this important sense.

Second, I would ask whether it is true that judges who reject literalism necessarily open the door to subjectivity. They do not endorse subjectivity. And under their approach important safeguards of objectivity remain. For one thing, a judge who emphasizes consequences, no less than any other, is aware of the legal precedents, rules, standards, practices, and institutional understanding that a decision will affect. He or she also takes account of the way in which this system of legally related rules, institutions, and practices affects the world.

To be sure, a court focused on consequences may decide a case in a way that radically changes the law. But this is not always a bad thing. For example, after the late-nineteenth-century Court decided *Plessy v. Ferguson,* the case which permitted racial segregation that was, in principle, "separate but equal," it became apparent that segregation did not mean equality but meant disrespect for members of a minority race and led to a segregated society that was totally unequal, a consequence directly contrary to the purpose and demands of the Fourteenth

Amendment. The Court, in *Brown v. Board of Education* and later decisions, overruled *Plessy*, and the law changed in a way that profoundly affected the lives of many.[10]

In any event, to focus upon consequences does not automatically invite frequent dramatic legal change. Judges, including those who look to consequences, understand the human need to plan in reliance upon law, the need for predictability, the need for stability. And they understand that too radical, too frequent legal change has, as a consequence, a tendency to undercut those important law-related human needs. Similarly, each judge's individual need to be consistent over time constrains subjectivity. As Justice O'Connor has explained, a constitutional judge's initial decisions leave "footprints" that the judge, in later decisions, will almost inevitably follow.[11]

Moreover, to consider consequences is not to consider simply whether the consequences of a proposed decision are good or bad, in a particular judge's opinion. Rather, to emphasize consequences is to emphasize consequences related to the particular textual provision at issue. The judge must examine the consequences through the lens of the relevant constitutional value or purpose. The relevant values limit interpretive possibilities. If they are democratic values, they may well counsel modesty or restraint as well. And I believe that when a judge candidly acknowledges that, in addition to text, history, and precedent, consequences also guide his decision-making, he is more likely to be disciplined in emphasizing, for example, constitutionally relevant consequences rather than allowing his own subjectively held values to be outcome determinative. In all these ways, a focus on consequences will itself constrain subjectivity.

Here are examples of how these principles apply. The First Amendment says that "Congress shall make no law respecting an establishment of religion." I recently wrote (in dissent) that this clause prohibits government from providing vouchers to parents to help pay for the education of their children in parochial schools. The basic reason, in my view, is that the clause seeks to avoid among other things the "social conflict, potentially created when government becomes involved in religious education." Nineteenth- and twentieth-century immigration has produced a nation with fifty or more different religions. And that fact made the risk of "social conflict" far more serious after the Civil War and in twentieth-century America than the Framers, with their eighteenth-century experience, might have anticipated. The twentieth-century Supreme Court had held in applicable precedent that, given the changing nature of our society, in order to implement the basic value that the Framers wrote the clause to protect, it was necessary to interpret the clause more broadly than the Framers might have thought likely.[12]

My opinion then turned to consequences. It said that voucher programs, if widely adopted, could provide billions of dollars to religious schools. At first blush, that may seem a fine idea. But will different religious groups become concerned about which groups are getting the money and how? What are the criteria? How are programs being implemented? Is a particular program biased against particular sects, say, because it forbids certain kinds of teaching? Are rival sects failing to live up to the relevant criteria, say, by teaching "civil disobedience" to "unjust laws"? How will claims for money, say, of one religious group against another, be adjudicated? In a society as religiously diverse as ours, I saw in the administration of huge grant programs for religious education the potential for religious strife. And that, it seemed to me, was the kind of problem the First Amendment's religion clauses seek to avoid.[13]

The same constitutional concern—the need to avoid a "divisiveness based upon religion that promotes social conflict"[14]—helped me determine whether the Establishment Clause forbade two public displays of the tablets of the Ten Commandments, one inside a Kentucky state courthouse, the other on the grounds of the Texas State Capitol. It is well recognized that the Establishment Clause does not allow the government to compel religious practices, to show favoritism among sects or between religion and non-religion, or to promote religion. Yet, at the same time, given the religious beliefs of most Americans, an absolutist approach that would purge all religious references from the public sphere could well promote the very kind of social conflict that the Establishment Clause seeks to avoid. Thus, I thought, the Establishment Clause cannot *automatically* forbid every public display of the Ten Commandments, despite the religious nature of its text. Rather, one must examine the context of the *particular* display to see whether, in that context, the tablets convey the kind of government-endorsed religious message that the Establishment Clause forbids.

The history of the Kentucky courthouse display convinced me and the other members of the Court's majority that the display sought to serve its sponsors' primarily religious objectives and that many of its viewers would understand it as reflecting that motivation. But the context of the Texas display differed significantly. A private civic (and primarily secular) organization had placed the tablets on the Capitol grounds as part of the organization's efforts to combat juvenile delinquency. Those grounds contained seventeen other monuments and twenty-one historical markers, none of which conveyed any religious message and all of which sought to illustrate the historical "ideals" of Texans. And the monument had stood for forty years without legal challenge. These circumstances strongly suggested that the public visiting the Capitol grounds had long considered the tablets' religious message as a secondary part of a broader moral and historical message reflecting a cultural heritage—a view of the display consistent with its promoters' basic objective.

It was particularly important that the Texas display stood uncontested for forty years. That fact indicated, as a practical matter of degree, that (unlike the Kentucky display) the Texas display was unlikely to prove socially divisive. Indeed, to require the display's removal itself would encourage disputes over the removal of long-standing depictions of the Ten Commandments from public buildings across the nation, thereby creating the very kind of religiously based divisiveness that the Establishment Clause was designed to prevent. By way of contrast, the short and stormy history of the more contemporary Kentucky display revealed both religious motivation and consequent social controversy. Thus, in the two cases, which I called borderline cases, consideration of likely consequences—evaluated in light of the purposes or values embodied within the Establishment Clause—helped produce a legal result: The Clause allowed the Texas display, while it forbade the display in Kentucky.

I am not arguing here that I was right in any of these cases. I am arguing that my opinions sought to identify a critical value underlying the Religion Clauses. They considered how that value applied in modern-day America; they looked for consequences relevant to that value. And they sought to evaluate likely consequences in terms of that value. That is what I mean by an interpretive approach that emphasizes consequences. Under that approach language, precedent, constitutional values, and factual circumstances all constrain judicial subjectivity.

Third, "subjectivity" is a two-edged criticism, which the literalist himself cannot escape. The literalist's tools—language and structure, history and tradition—often fail to provide objective guidance in those truly difficult cases about which I have spoken. Will canons of interpretation provide objective answers? One canon tells the court to choose an interpretation that gives every statutory word a meaning. Another permits the court to ignore a word, treating it as surplus, if otherwise the construction is repugnant to the statute's purpose. Shall the court read the statute narrowly as in keeping with the common law or broadly as remedial in purpose? Canons to the left of them, canons to the right of them, which canons shall the judges choose to follow?[15]

Recall the case about the Foreign Sovereign Immunities Act, in which the question was whether the statutory word "control" has a broad or a narrow meaning. Should the Court, choosing a narrow meaning, have emphasized Congress's use of a different phrase *"direct or indirect control"* in other statutes where it intended a broad meaning? Or should it instead have emphasized Congress's use of the same phrase—the single word "control"—in a yet different set of statutes where Congress also intended a broad meaning? Or should it have counted how many times Congress did each? Why place greater weight on the canon suggesting a need to give every statutory word a separate meaning than upon the statute's overall purpose?

Recall *Chevron*. Reference to the hypothetical reasonable member of Congress introduces no more subjectivity than the Court's own efforts to construct workable interpretive rules without any such reference. On both views *Chevron* requires courts to decide when an agency interpretation is reasonable—thereby opening the door to subjectivity.

Consider a recent Ex Post Facto Clause case from our Court. We had to decide whether the clause barred California from enacting a new statute of limitations, applying it retroactively, and then prosecuting an individual for child molestation twenty years after the old limitations period had expired. The Court used one of the literalist's tools, history, to find the answer. Two hundred years ago, Justice Chase, borrowing Blackstone's three-centuries-old language, had said the Ex Post Facto Clause was applicable when, for example, a law made a crime "greater than" it previously was. Did California's retroactive statute of limitations make the crime "greater than" it previously was?[16]

The answer, historically speaking, depended upon the nature of certain events in England that inspired Blackstone's formulation. All members of the Court carefully examined two abusive parliamentary prosecutions of 350 years ago—those of the Earl of Clarendon and the Bishop of Atterbury. Everyone agreed that the Ex Post Facto Clause barred prosecutions of the kind at issue in those cases. But there the agreement ended. The dissent thought that these historic parliamentary prosecutions had nothing to do with the case at hand. The majority thought that they offered it considerable support. Who was right? The truthful answer—and one I believe a reading of the opinions will support—is that no one but an expert historian could possibly know. And even the experts might disagree. Judges are not expert historians. How does reliance upon history bring about certainty or objectivity in such a case?[17]

Why do I point out the uncertainties, in close cases, of linguistic structure, of canons of interpretation, and of history? Because those difficulties mean that the "textualist," "originalist," and "literalist" approaches themselves possess inherently subjective elements. Which linguistic characteristics are determinative? Which canons shall we choose? Which historical account shall we use? Which tradition shall we apply? And how does that history, or that tradition, apply now?

Significantly, an effort to answer these questions can produce a decision that is not only subjective but also *unclear*, lacking transparency about the factors that the judge considers truly significant. A decision that directly addresses consequences, purposes, and values is no more subjective, at worst, and has the added value of exposing underlying judicial motivations, specifying the points of doubt for all to read. This is particularly important because transparency of rationale permits informed public criticism of opinions; and that criticism, in a democracy, plays an important role in checking abuse of judicial power.

Fourth, I do not believe that textualist or originalist methods of interpretation are more likely to produce clear, workable legal rules. But even were they to do so, the advantages of legal rules can be overstated. Rules must be interpreted and applied. Every law student whose class grade is borderline knows that the benefits that rules produce for cases that fall within the heartland are often lost in cases that arise at the boundaries.

Nor is clarity exclusively promoted through use of rules. Metaphors and examples also can illuminate. Section 3 of the Clayton Act, for example, prohibits a seller from making a sale on the condition that the buyer will "not use or deal in the goods... of [the seller's] competitor." This language most obviously applies to a seller who actually exacts a promise from his buyers. But it also captures cases in which the seller conditions the sale of one product on the buyer's purchasing a different product as well. The courts have introduced the metaphor of "tying" to describe this practice. In doing so, they have made the scope of the statute's proscription more vivid and concrete to the benefit of lawyers, businesses, and courts alike. The common law, too, has long set forth law by way of example—embodied in the facts of the individual case. That precedent has guided ordinary buyers and sellers, promoting prosperity through greater commercial certainty, for close to three centuries.[18]

In any event, insistence upon clear rules can exact a high constitutional price. California enacted a high-penalty mandatory sentencing law, "three strikes and you're out." California, applying this law, imposed a fifty-year sentence on an individual whose third crime was stealing $153 worth of videotapes; it imposed a twenty-five-year sentence on another individual whose third crime was theft of several golf clubs. Our Court had to decide whether these sentences violated the Constitution's Cruel and Unusual Punishment Clause, a question that turned on whether the sentences were "grossly disproportionate." The majority thought not, with some Justices expressing concern about the workability of any contrary holding.[19]

I was in the minority. I conceded that striking down the law would leave the Court without a clear rule that would readily distinguish those sentences that are "grossly disproportionate" from those that are not. Courts might have to exercise judgment in each case. But that judgment would not lack guidance. A Supreme Court opinion, based on examples, discussing how, and why, the standard applied to the cases before us would help to provide that guidance. Regardless, the administrative gains from rule-based clarity were not worth the constitutional price. Insisting on a clear rule has made the clause virtually inapplicable to any specific-length prison sentence.[20]

Fifth, textualist and originalist doctrines may themselves produce seriously harmful consequences—outweighing whatever risks of subjectivity or uncertainty are inherent in other approaches. I have deliberately chosen examples to illustrate that harm. In respect to statutory interpretation, a canon-based approach meant more complex jurisdictional law that closed the federal courthouse doors to certain foreign state-owned enterprises, thereby increasing foreign relations friction, just what Congress enacted the statute (the Foreign Sovereign Immunities Act) to avoid. Emphasizing a statute's literal language meant a habeas corpus law that randomly closes the doors of federal courts to a set of state prisoners. In respect to administrative law, a canonlike interpretation of *Chevron* risks judicial deference to an agency interpretation of a statute in circumstances in which no reasonable legislator could have so intended, thereby substituting an agency view of the statute for an interpretation likely more consistent with the views of the public's elected representatives.

In respect to the First Amendment, a more textualist (if not more originalist) approach would treat all speech alike—"speech is speech and that is the end of the matter." The compound drug example showed that application of such a view could unreasonably impede reasonable health-based regulatory objectives. In respect to federalism, a more originalist approach could impede efforts to draw citizens into local administration of federal programs—thereby inhibiting the development of a cooperative federalism that can mean more effective regulatory programs consistent with constitutional design. In Eleventh Amendment cases, that approach (if, indeed, the Court's approach can be called originalist) would prevent

Congress from creating uniform national remedies in such areas as protection of intellectual property—an area in which modern global commercial circumstances make uniform enforcement methods important, if not a necessity.

In respect to privacy, a more literal, less consequence-oriented, approach would not necessarily value the reasons for judicial hesitation, thereby taking inadequate account of ongoing legislative processes and consequently leading to premature judicial interference with legislative development. In respect to equal protection, a more literal approach could have read the Equal Protection Clause divisively, impeding rather than furthering the democratic unity needed to make the Constitution's institutions work as intended.

Of course, my examples are no more than that, examples. They do not prove the general superiority of the interpretations they illustrate. But if one agrees that an examination of consequences can help us determine whether our interpretations promote specific democratic purposes and general constitutional objectives, I will have made my point. That point is that a more literal approach has serious drawbacks. Whatever "subjectivity-limiting" benefits a more literal, textual, or originalist approach may bring, and I believe those benefits are small, it will also bring with it serious accompanying consequential harm.

Much of the harm at stake is a constitutional harm. Literalism has a tendency to undermine the Constitution's efforts to create a framework for democratic government—a government that, while protecting basic individual liberties, permits citizens to govern themselves, and to govern themselves effectively. In so far as a more literal interpretive approach undermines this basic objective, it is inconsistent with the most fundamental original intention of the Framers themselves.

For any or all of these reasons, I hope that those strongly committed to textualist or literalist views—those whom I am almost bound not to convince—are fairly small in number. I hope to have convinced some of the rest that active liberty has an important role to play in constitutional (and statutory) interpretation.

That role, I repeat, does not involve radical change in current professional interpretive methods nor does it involve ignoring the protection the Constitution grants fundamental (modern) liberties. It takes Thomas Jefferson's statement as a statement of goals that the Constitution now seeks to fulfill: "[A]ll men are created equal." They are endowed by their Creator with certain "unalienable Rights." "[T]o secure these Rights, Governments are instituted among Men, *deriving their just powers from the consent of the governed*." It underscores, emphasizes, or reemphasizes the final democratic part of the famous phrase. That reemphasis, I believe, has practical value when judges seek to assure fidelity, in our modern society, to these ancient and unchanging ideals.[21]

There is another reason, a practical reason, for insisting upon the constitutional importance of democratic self-government. We are all aware of figures that show that the public knows ever less about, and is ever less interested in, the processes of government. Foundation reports criticize the lack of high school civics education. A credible national survey reveals that more students know the names of the Three Stooges than the three branches of government. Law school graduates are ever less inclined to work for government—with the percentage of those entering government work (or nongovernment public interest work) declining at one major law school from 12 per cent to 3 per cent over the course of a generation. Polling figures suggest that during that same time, the percentage of the public trusting the government has declined at a similar rate.[22]

This trend, however, is not irreversible. Indeed, trust in government, and interest in public service, showed a remarkable rebound in response to the terrorist attacks of September 11, 2001. Courts alone cannot maintain the rebound. Indeed, judges cannot easily advocate the virtues of democracy. But they need not do so. Americans already accept as theirs those democratic virtues and objectives to which Tocqueville once pointed: not spiritual "loftiness," a "contempt for material goods," elevated "manners," "poetry, renown, glory," the "most glory possible," but "reason," "peaceful habits," "well being," a "prosperous society" whose "energy . . . can bring forth marvels."[23]

Still, courts, as highly trusted government institutions, might help in various ways. Judges can explain in terms the public can understand just what the Constitution is about. They can make clear, above all, that the Constitution is not a document designed to solve the problems of a community at any level—local, state, or national. Rather it is a document that trusts people to solve those problems themselves. And it creates a *framework* for a government that will help them do so. That framework foresees democratically determined solutions, protective of the individual's basic liberties. It assures each individual that the law will treat him or her with equal respect. It seeks a form of democratic government that will prove workable over time.[24]

This is the democratic ideal. It is as relevant today as it was two hundred or two thousand years ago. More than two thousand years ago, Thucydides quoted Pericles as telling his fellow Athenians: "We do not say that the man who fails to participate in politics is a man who minds his own business. We say that he is a man who has no business here." Related ideals, the sharing of political authority, a free people delegating that authority to a democratically elected government, participation by those people in that democratic process, moved the Framers. And they wrote a Constitution that embodied these ideals. We judges cannot insist that Americans participate in that government. But we can make clear that our Constitution depends upon it. Their participation is necessary. It is a critical part of that "positive passion for the public good" that John Adams, like so many others, believed was a necessary condition for any "real Liberty" and for the "Republican Government" that the Constitution creates.[25]

CHAPTER NINE

A BROADER APPLICATION

This book is about an American Constitution and its interpretation by American judges. In that context it discusses the role of active liberty, while emphasizing the importance of purpose and consequences when judges interpret ambiguous legal texts. The American context, however, has become ever less special. The citizens of nations throughout the world treasure democracy. They seek to protect basic human rights. Increasingly nations have embodied these ideals in legal documents. And increasingly they have given independent judiciaries authority to enforce those legal texts. These similarities mean that the book's discussion should have broader application in today's interconnected world. And I have chosen three examples to suggest that the book's themes have relevance outside the United States.

My first example focuses upon the Turkish headscarf case in the European Court of Human Rights. I find parallels between that case and the American "affirmative action" case that I earlier discussed. And I suggest that "active liberty" might play a similarly useful analytic role in both instances. My second example considers the institutions of the European Union. I suggest that the EU's "democratic deficit" complicates the judges' task in applying the EU's governing documents with appropriate judicial restraint. The "democratic deficit" thereby threatens to place the European Court of Justice in an awkward judicial dilemma of a kind that on historical occasion the American Supreme Court has also had to face.

My third example returns to an American problem with foreign implications, our Supreme Court's practice of referring in its own decisions to foreign law and the decisions of courts in other nations. I believe the example will show the importance of a form of legal analysis that emphasizes purposes, values and consequences.

The headscarf, religious freedom, and active liberty

Article 9 of the European Convention on Human Rights guarantees each individual "the right" of "freedom of...religion," a right that "includes" the individual's "freedom...in public or private, to manifest" his or her "religion or belief, in worship, teaching, practice and observance." Turkish law prohibits women from wearing religious headscarves at state universities. And the European Court of Human Rights, in *Leyla Şahin v. Turkey,* considered and rejected the claim of a religious Turkish medical student that this Turkish law violates Article 9.[1]

The Court found that the law restricts religious freedom. But it found the restriction justified. Article 9 explicitly states that "freedom of thought, conscience, and religion" are "subject . . . to . . . limitations," but "only" to those limitations that "are *necessary in a democratic society* in the interests of public safety, for the protection of public order, health or morals or for the protection of the rights and freedoms of others." The Court, in reaching its conclusion, applied a "margin of appreciation" to the Turkish law. That is to say, the Court conducted its assessment of the Turkish law's validity deferentially, reading the Convention as providing individual nations with a degree of legislative leeway within which the Court must accept as binding a nation's own judgment that its law conforms to the Convention's requirements. And the Court concluded that Turkey's law, so viewed, was (in the Convention's words) "necessary in a democratic society . . . for the protection of public order" and "for the protection of the rights and freedoms of others."

The Court marshaled several considerations in support of its conclusion. It indicated that that the Turkish legal principle of "secularism" (a) prevents "the State from manifesting a preference for a particular religion or belief," (b) requires the State to assume the "role of impartial arbiter," and (c) serves "to protect the individual . . . from external pressure from extremist movements." The Court added that "in the Turkish context," where a majority of citizens adhere to the Islamic faith, the wearing of an Islamic headscarf "as a compulsory religious duty" may have a negative impact "on those who choose not to wear it." In fact the wearing of the headscarf in Turkey had recently "taken on political significance" and "extremist political movements" sought "to impose on society as a whole their religious symbols and conception of a society founded on religious precepts." The Court concluded that these circumstances taken together with the Convention's principle of "gender equality" satisfy Article 9's demand for justification. Thus the four considerations just mentioned, taken together with the "margin of appreciation," outweigh the restriction's negative effect upon an individual's religious liberty.[2]

Let us now re-consider these factors, this time viewing them through the lens of active liberty. In doing so, I shall suggest that concept of active liberty might shed additional light on the legal analysis.

As the Court recognized, the principle of secularism, European practice, and precedent, taken alone, cannot justify Turkey's law. The Turkish secularism principle (*"laik,"* in Turkish), if similar to the French principle of *laicité,* seeks to draw a clear line between a non-religious state sector and a potentially religious private sector. The State embodies secularity in much the way that the pre-Revolutionary French State embodied Catholicism. A state official uttering a public prayer amounts to a virtual contradiction in terms. And, in this sense, the Turkish or French law extends beyond that of Britain, which finds religious freedom compatible with an established church. They also extend beyond the law of the United States, which reads its constitutional prohibition of religious establishment in a practical conflict-minimizing way, hence as assuring a state neutrality that could prove compatible with, say, opening a legislative session with a prayer.

Yet the Turkish women who wish to wear religious headscarves are not government officials nor do they engage in governmental activity. The claimant, Leyla Şahin, is a private citizen, a fifth-year medical student, who wishes to wear the headscarf when she attends lectures. And the headscarf prohibition has forced her to complete her medical studies outside Turkey, in Vienna, where she can wear the scarf.

Nor have many other nations found the wearing of a headscarf incompatible with a strict secularism principle. Of the forty-six nations subscribing to the Convention only Turkey, Azerbaijan and Albania have enacted a headscarf prohibition. The Court wrote, "In Austria, Germany, the Netherlands, Spain, Sweden, Switzerland, and the United Kingdom (in some cases following a protracted legal debate) the state education authorities permit Muslim pupils and students to wear the Islamic headscarf.... In a number of other countries (the Czech Republic, Greece, Hungary, Poland or Slovakia), the wearing of the Islamic headscarf does not yet appear to have given rise to any detailed legal debate." French law provides support for the Turkish position in so far as the law in France prohibits "the wearing of signs or dress by which pupils manifest a religious affiliation." But the French prohibition applies only in primary and secondary schools, where the children are younger and the State arguably possesses a stronger interest in shaping the instructional environment.[3]

Neither can the Court rest its conclusion upon legal precedent. The Court found support for its conclusion in two cases, *Karaduman v. Turkey* and *Dahlab v. Switzerland*. But the first of these cases held only that universities may prevent certain fundamentalist religious movements from exerting pressure on those who do not practice their religion, a pressure that Leyla Şahin (whom no one claims is a fundamentalist) said she did not intend to exert. And the second case concerned the wearing of headscarves by teachers, who were state officials, not by university students. Precedent established only that it is *sometimes* permissible for a state university to regulate the religious activities of university students, not that it is permissible in present circumstances.[4]

Not surprisingly, the Court went on to refer to other factors. It discussed the margin of appreciation. It mentioned the principle of "gender equality." It noted that the wearing of headscarves had taken on "political significance." And it emphasized that Turkey's ban on the wearing of religious headscarves would help prevent religious students from putting pressure upon non-religious students to wear headscarves as well. Might the concept of active liberty prove helpful in evaluating these latter considerations?

A Broader Application

As I have explained, the concept of active liberty is about democracy. It reflects each citizen's right to share in the determination of a community's rules, laws, and policies. And it foresees the citizen's active participation in that process. The Convention frequently refers to democracy. Articles 6, 8, 9, 10, and 11 repeatedly insist that legal limitations upon basic liberty are justified only where those limitations are "necessary in a democratic society." In fact, Article 9 does not authorize a legal restriction on religious freedom, such as the headscarf law, simply because it helps to "protect[]...the rights and freedoms of others." But rather Article 9 insists that any "limitation[]" on religious freedom be "necessary...*in a democratic society*" to provide that "protection." Is the headscarf law "necessary" in Turkey's "*democratic society*" to protect an ordinary non-religious student from pressure by religious students? The language invites a consideration of democracy itself.

The "margin of appreciation," upon which the Court heavily relies, to some degree reflects democratic considerations. The notion recognizes that different cultural, historical, and political backgrounds of the forty-six different Convention nations make certain restrictions more acceptable in some nations than in others. It recognizes that, in Europe, it is the individual nation that legislates democratically, not the Council of Europe. And judicial respect for democracy consequently requires the Court to provide democratically elected national legislatures with a degree of legal leeway, even where resulting laws arguably restrict the rights of some citizens. But there is more. As soon as I start to examine the headscarf issue from a democratic perspective, I begin to think of the American "affirmative action" case that I discussed earlier. In that case the American Constitution's assumption of workable democracy helped resolve a constitutional problem of discrimination. The principle of active liberty favored interpreting the Constitution's anti-discrimination clause as permitting a degree of affirmative action thereby encouraging the participation of all citizens, including those of minority race, in American society. A similar assumption (favoring inclusion) about the words "necessary in a democratic society" might help analyze a Convention-related problem of religious freedom. That assumption would lead us to ask: To what extent will the University's "no headscarf" rule help to assure women's participation in Turkey's secular democratic system of government? Perhaps the question is implicit in the European Court's reference to "extremist political movements" that seek to impose their religious views on a secular society.

Where does the question lead? On the one hand, one might plausibly claim that a permissive rule allowing headscarves would bring about their widespread use by more religious Turkish women, consequently discouraging less religious Turkish women from attending class with heads bare and thereby helping to bring about a more religiously-oriented university atmosphere. Such an atmosphere would, in turn, lead some of those women to adopt (perhaps with serious reservations) a more traditional, less participatory role in society. On the other hand, one might plausibly assert that where as here the challenged rule applies to adult medical school students, the university is secular, and the university has long operated without a headscarf ban, the empirical links just sketched are far-fetched—even taking a "margin of appreciation" into account. The question does not tell us how to decide the case; but it does tell us where to look for empirical help. In that way the democratic question transforms the case. It focuses upon empirical matters—matters that lend themselves to resolution through consideration of fact, experience, and evidence.

The European Court's headscarf opinion (unlike my own Court's affirmative action opinion) did not focus directly upon those empirical matters. That fact may simply reflect a reluctance of the parties before the Court to bolster their claims with empirical evidence or experience-based opinion. The parties and other groups that appeared before our Court in the affirmative action case showed no such reluctance.

Would greater emphasis upon evidence—about the relation of the headscarf law to Turkey's democratic political circumstances—have led the Court to a different conclusion in the particular case? The dissenting judge

ACTIVE LIBERTY

believed it would. The dissent insisted that Turkey provide stronger evidentiary justification for its ban— evidence that would support the existence of genuine empirical links between the headscarf ban and the public harms the ban sought to prevent. In the absence of that evidence, the dissenting judge would have found Turkey's law incompatible with the Convention.

But even if Turkey could not provide sufficient empirical support for its justification in the particular case, a different conclusion in the particular case would not have required the Court to strike down anti-headscarf laws across the board. Nor would it have required the Court to narrow significantly the "margin of appreciation" that it applies to Turkey's legislative decision-making. That is because special facts of the case permit a carefully limited holding. The case before the Court involved 1) an adult medical student, who 2) was a sincere religious believer, but 3) was not a pros-elytizer 4) nor a fundamentalist, where the medical student 5) did not wear the headscarf as a political provocation, and whom 6) the ban harmed significantly by requiring her to attend a medical school outside the country. A ruling that found the Convention and Turkey's law incompatible, by emphasizing any, or all, of these special circumstances, would have returned the matter to Turkey's legislature and to Turkey's political processes. It would have allowed Turkey to enact further, more tailored headscarf legislation provided that Turkey could show a reasonable democrat-ically-related need for the headscarf law.

A Broader Application

Focus upon the democratic question might have led to several conclusions: the "no headscarf" rule seriously limits religious freedom; any such limitation requires strong justification; but the need to assure an equal opportunity for women to participate in a democratic society can (if shown) provide that justification. Moreover, the transformation of a value-laden question into a primarily empirical question can help to preserve the appearance (and reality) of judicial impartiality—an important consideration in a court with judges of different cultural backgrounds who seek to apply the Convention's basic, general, value-laden provisions to a multi-cultural society.

I leave it to others, however, to evaluate the Court's decision in the particular case. My object here is only to illustrate a possible connection between two cases from two different jurisdictions, the affirmative action case in the United States and the headscarf case in Strasbourg. And in doing so, I hope to show a connection between a Convention that speaks of a democratic society and the concept of active liberty.

Active liberty and the European Union

My second example focuses upon the European Union and its governing institutions. I shall describe those institutions, emphasizing the complexities that surround the EU's democratic roots. Those complexities create legal tensions that can make the work of a court, such as the European Court of Justice, more difficult. By showing how the *absence* of clarity (in respect to democracy) complicates the Court's interpretative task, I hope to illustrate an additional aspect of active liberty's jurisprudential value. The European Union treaties create complex lines of authority between EU decision-makers and citizens. The treaties establish four basic institutions: a Council, a Commission, a Parliament, and a Court. The *Council* is a kind of legislature. Each Member State has one vote. Each State's Prime Minister (or other Member State government representative) may attend and cast that vote at Council meetings.

The *Commission* is, in effect, a group of administrators. Each Member State government selects one Commissioner. But the Commissioners see themselves, not as representing a Member State or a political party, but as managing a department of civil servants responsible for, e.g., transport, communications, competition policy, and so forth.

The *Parliament* is a legislative institution. Its Members, elected from districts, have organized themselves roughly speaking by political party. But the Parliament is an unusual legislative body in that it cannot initiate legislation. Rather it simply has a veto over some, but not all, legislation that the Commission proposes. Still, because its approval is needed for most legislation (but not where the subject matter is agriculture, budget or foreign trade), the Parliament can negotiate with the Council in order to bring about laws more to its liking.

A Broader Application

The *Court*, which sits in Luxembourg, has twenty-five members who serve for a term of seven years. Each Member State selects one judge. The Court authoritatively interprets EU law, and it determines whether the laws of Member States conflict with EU law.

In his introduction to the recently proposed EU Constitution, Giscard d'Estaing explains the original structure of the EU, then the Common Market, as follows: the Commission was to be an administrative body with exclusive authority to propose legislation (seeking the best interests of the European Community); the Parliament would provide advice to the Council; the Council, acting as the EU's legislature, would decide whether to enact the legislation the Commission had proposed. Subsequent treaties have modified this original structure, for example, by granting the Parliament the veto power that I have described.

Inherent in the EU's complex institutional structure are two serious democratic problems. The first arises out of a basic ambiguity in the connection between EU policy and the average voter. What route is the line of democratic legitimating authority supposed to take? Does it run from the EU decision maker through an elected EU Parliament to the voter? Or does it run from the EU decision maker through the Member State Governments and their own Member State Government elections to the voter? The more one sees the EU Parliament as primary legislator, the more one emphasizes the first line of authority; the more one sees the EU Council as primary legislator, the more one emphasizes the second line of authority. Taken together the two separate lines of authority are in tension.

One cannot wish away the tension by claiming that the EU is simply a trade treaty and that the Council simply provides its Member States a way to agree as to how to implement or to modify that treaty (sometimes unanimously, sometimes by weighted majority). The other EU bodies are too numerous, their authority too significant, and the Council's own powers too limited, to make any such analogy plausible.

Nor can one wish away the democratic tension by claiming that the Council is a kind of upper legislative house, like the United States Senate. The Council's Members do not see themselves as individual Senators; they are *governments*. And Member State votes in Council reflect that fact. Unlike an individual Senator, whose electorate holds him or her responsible for Senate votes and little else, the electorate of a Member State Government holds that Government responsible for much more than its EU activity, diminishing the visibility of the democratic link between electorate and Council vote. In any event, since 1913 individual citizens, not state legislatures, have elected United States Senators. Most importantly, the Council and the Parliament event taken together lack full legislative powers. They cannot initiate legislation. They can only enact (or refuse to enact) legislation that the Commission will propose.

A Broader Application

The second problem is raised by the Commission's powers. That body is meant to be "independent" while also possessing the sole power to initiate legislation. Indeed, Commissioners enjoy a greater legal independence than most of their American administrative counterparts. No President or Prime Minister or Council can easily dismiss them. Nor can the public. I concede that Parliament possesses a dismissal power. And by insisting upon the appointment of a Commission to its policy liking (say as the British Parliament did in the eighteenth century), it might transform the Commission into a form of Parliamentary Executive. But Parliament has not yet exercised its dismissal power for policy-related purposes. How then is a vote in a national or in a European election to bring about a policy change that requires the initiation of legislation?

These circumstances raise a classical dilemma of government and administrative law: Who will regulate the regulators? How are the people to control administrators who are themselves not elected? How will a vote in either an EU or a national election bring about policy change? Is it sufficient to require Parliament and the Council to concur with the Commission in order to bring about change, or does that requirement simply freeze in place the status quo? The voter likely does not know the answer to these questions.

In America in the 1930s, when Franklin Roosevelt's New Deal expanded the role of the federal government, many scholars answered this question with the words "expert discipline." Just as the rules, canons, skills and professional understandings of the doctor, lawyer, or engineer set standards for their behavior, so technical standards would control those who practice, for example, the "science" of railroad rate-setting. By the 1970s, however, few scholars considered rate-setting (or other administrative tasks) an exact professional discipline capable of setting standards that could effectively control the actions of administrators. Rather, we now see value judgements and political judgements as permeating the administrators' work. And so the American legal system has developed other methods of control—political control through congressional hearings and budgeting as well as presidential appointment of regulators; judicial control through court review of agency action; and direct democratic control through public participation in "notice-and-comment" rulemaking.

The EU system seems to present the central dilemma of administrative law yet more forcefully. The EU has developed certain systems of control, including a requirement of Parliamentary (and Council) agreement to bring about changes in (certain) law; a degree of judicial review, Parliamentary hearings and budgeting, and Member State appointment of Commissioners. Are these systems of control sufficient? Should we view Commissioners and their civil servants as experts whose actions are also subject to the controls of an expert discipline? Or should we view them as public policy makers whose actions (or decisions *not* to act) should be subject to political controls? Because the United States has not found perfect solutions to its own similar problems, many Americans will watch with interest as the European Union seeks answers.

Of course, the detailed workings of every government are complex and the power relationships in practice often differ from those set forth in governing documents. But in the case of the EU the governing documents themselves set forth many of the ambiguities, uncertainties and complexities I have described. That fact makes it particularly difficult to trace the authoritative connections between policy decision and voter. It increases the democratic distance between policy and voter. It makes it less likely that a voter will understand the policy implications—in terms of subsequent rules, regulations, or Commission-proposed legislation—of his or her vote for one Euro-party, or one Member State party, rather than another. To put the matter colloquially, an average, even a well informed, voter (say a voter dissatisfied with basic EU policies and wishing change) is uncertain how to answer a basic democratic question: How can we throw the rascals out? That is the democratic dilemma.

This institutional complexity and the democratic uncertainty that it creates may pose special problems for judges, in particular for the European Court of Justice when it seeks to interpret the treaties, laws, and regulations. I shall provide three illustrations of interpretive obstacles that the judges might overcome more easily were the European Union's foundation in democratic principle, i.e. "active liberty," more certain.

My first example arises out of the fact that the basic European legal texts, e.g., the treaties, are ambiguous in respect to ultimate objectives. It is difficult for the Court to construct a unified approach to interpretation—an approach through which a single aim, or a single coherent set of aims, might inform the interpretation of a document's myriad individual provisions. The treaties do refer to democracy. Article F of Title I of the Maastricht Treaty refers to the fact that the Governments of the Member States are "founded on the principles of democracy." And the Preamble to the Charter of Fundamental Rights says that the "Union... is based on the principles of democracy." But the Charter's legal role is limited. And one cannot describe the creation of democratic institutions as the EU's central aim.[5]

At one time, the EU's governing documents pointed generally towards a different aim, advancing a single overall EU objective: increased freedom of trade. Thus, one can imagine a basic interpretive approach that roughly reflected the Court's determination to scrutinize closely Member State legislation that potentially interfered with free trade, the basic EU objective, but to examine less strictly other forms of Member State legislation. Now, however, the EU's governing documents, which include a (non-binding) Charter of Human Rights, point beyond free trade to other basic objectives, both protection of individual rights and certain forms of social democracy, i.e., a society that guarantees economic and social minima. (The proposed Constitution with its mandatory Human Rights Charter would have gone farther in this latter direction.)

The jurisprudential difficulty arises out of the fact that free trade and social democracy, while often in harmony, sometimes conflict. When they diverge, the Court must choose the predominant value. Which shall it be? The documents themselves do not tell us. Nor, given the democratic difficulties that I have described, can the Court look to principles of active liberty for help. (Compare the manner in which reference to those values helped our Court, see, e.g., Chapter Two). In so far as the Court cannot read the EU's foundational document as providing clear democratic instructions, it will find it correspondingly more difficult to make value choices of the kind just mentioned.

The second example shows how difficult it is for judges to define a "margin of appreciation," a degree of deference towards, for example, administrators, without an underlying basic legal text that incorporates fundamental democratic values. Suppose the Court were faced with some of the privacy/new technology issues that I discussed earlier. Imagine that: 1) An EU privacy regulation seeking to protect cell-phone conversations penalizes a newspaper editor for publishing important information obtained through the unlawful interception of such a call. 2) An EU privacy regulation forbids the compelled disclosure of an individual's genetic make-up—even where such disclosure would save a relative's life. 3) An EU privacy regulation forbids firms to use internet-obtained customer information for commercial purposes—even if the customer clicks a box signaling consent.

I have explained why American courts, faced with comparable examples, can take comfort in the fact that the laws in question arose out of public debate, a kind of local, state and national conversation, in which ordinary citizens can (and do) take part. Those laws were enacted through a legislative process, open to public participation, or an administrative process subject to the control of public officials, for both of which the voter must ultimately take responsibility. These democratic circumstances mean that courts often can defer to legislatures, asking not whether the laws in question represent the wisest policy but whether they fall outside the broad boundaries that the Constitution draws around the legislative process.

Can the European Court similarly defer to Commission and Council decisions? Were the matter primarily scientific or technical, it might defer to the Commission for technical reasons, i.e., because the Commission typically can draw upon greater specialized expertise than can the court. But the questions that I have mentioned are not purely technical. Important value judgments lie at their heart: For example, free expression versus privacy, privacy versus life, improved production versus consumer protection. A technical Commission of civil servants possesses no special insight about how to weigh these competing values.

The Council, aware of these problems, sometimes provides a degree of supervision over the Commission, through the use of specialized Council committees that interact with the Commission or its staff. Moreover, the Council may seek itself to enact regulations that have a significant value element. Thus, the Court may grant regulations a degree of leeway, on the theory that either the regulation is technical, enacted by experts, or it is value laden enacted by democratically-responsive bodies (Council and Parliament). Yet the Commission retains the initiating power; it is not always easy to separate a technical regulation from a value-laden regulation; and the democratic link between Council and people remains indirect and distant. Thus it remains debatable whether the European Court should grant the Council and Commission the kind of leeway that American courts typically grant to Congress or state legislatures.

Were the Commission (or Council) a forum for participatory public debate or were its decisions reflective of such debate elsewhere, say in the European Parliament, the Court then might defer to the decisions of that body for democratic reasons, as American courts might defer to the decisions of Congress or its agencies or of state legislatures. But the democratic problems I earlier discussed render somewhat hollow the suggestion that the Court defer to the Commission or to the Council or to Parliament for democratic reasons, particularly if the Court considers a Commission regulation to which the Council has paid little attention. The less convincing the democratic rationale for deference, the less likely the Court will provide it.

The third example concerns the classic democratic problem of judicial review, namely the need to justify (or to keep within reasonable bounds) in a democracy the power of unelected judges to make binding decisions. The EU judges of the EU Court in Luxembourg are not elected. Hence the problem exists. And certain features of the EU's policy-making institutions aggravate the problem.

In particular, current EU rules require the Council to take many of its decisions by unanimous vote rather than by "weighted voting," i.e., a form of voting that gives greater weight to States with greater population. Some Member States have favored unanimity and opposed the use of "weighted voting" for too many decisions, on the ground that unanimity helps to strengthen and to preserve the State's own democratically-based internal authority to make laws. Yet a rule requiring Council unanimity to act in a particular area automatically requires Council unanimity to overturn a Court decision in that area. Were the Council to oppose, for example, a Court interpretation of an EU rule or regulation in that area, it could not change it by a weighted majority vote. There is irony in the fact that the more the Member States seek to protect democratically-enacted national laws from EU interference by increasing the area within which the Council needs unanimous agreement to legislate, the more difficult it becomes to overturn a decision of the undemocratically-selected European Court, in effect granting that Court considerably more power to control the legislative agenda than is possessed by the Supreme Court of most nations (including my own). The Court is aware of the problem, and its knowledge that its interpretations cannot be changed may lead to a more cautious jurisprudence.

My basic point is a jurisprudential point. I focus on the judicial difficulty of applying constitutional provisions that guarantee modern liberty (i.e., liberty from governmental interference) along with protection of social and economic rights, but which do not similarly guarantee ancient liberty, the right to participate actively in democratic government. I emphasize the words "judicial difficulty" to make clear that my discussion involves institutional details that might well be modified as political conditions permit. Nor do I suggest that American courts have found satisfactory answers to similar questions. Rather, in a world where problems of commercial trade, immigration, and human liberty have impact beyond national borders, American observers will look on with interest as Europeans develop solutions to problems that resemble their own.

In pointing to the interpretive difficulties that a court might face, I do not deny the numerous ways in which EU institutions embody democratic principles. Nor am I advocating change in the basic nature of the European enterprise. Anyone who can remember the history of the last century must hope for the success of that enterprise. Rather, while basing my observations upon American experience, I am trying to show a modern need in all our nations to consider where and how institutions of government rest upon a democratic base, to urge the importance of democratic participation, and to illustrate how clarity in this respect can help to promote the development of more coherent interpretation of fundamental law, including the fundamental law of Europe.

Purpose, consequence and "foreign law"

Earlier I considered active liberty as part of a broader interpretive tradition. That tradition relies less heavily upon a text's formal qualities, such as literal language or interpretive canons, and more heavily upon the text's purposes and related consequences. My third example concerns the work of foreign courts. It focuses upon what Professor Gustavo Zagrebelsky, a former President of the Italian Constitutional Court, has called the "controversy regarding the use and citing by... courts of 'external' normative and jurisprudential materials." It illustrates how the purposive tradition might help to alleviate the "controversy."

The "problem" of American court references to foreign law is, in fact, two separate problems. The first is politically exciting, highly controversial, and, in my view, not of great importance. The second is more mundane, less politically visible, hardly controversial, and, in my view, highly important.

Two recent Supreme Court cases, *Lawrence v. Texas* and *Roper v. Simmons,* illustrate the first problem. In *Lawrence* the Court struck down a state law criminalizing certain forms of homosexual conduct, and it supported its decision in part by referring to a somewhat similar case from the European Court of Human Rights. In *Roper* the Court struck down state laws that would have applied the death penalty to sixteen- or seventeen-year-old defendants (convicted of capital murder), and it supported its decision in part by referring to the fact that no other nation applied a death penalty to offenders under the age of eighteen.[6]

The Court's references to foreign law in these cases immediately sparked public controversy. Dissenting justices as well as several commentators criticized the Court's referring to foreign decisions in support of its decision. And forty Members of Congress introduced legislation that would severely limit federal courts' use of foreign law in deciding constitutional issues. Since that time judges and commentators alike have engaged in debate. Indeed, my colleague Justice Scalia and I have debated the issue in opinions and at law school forums.

Those favoring the foreign-reference practice point to historical precedent. They add that the decisions of foreign courts do not bind us. And they argue that, in an ever more democratic world with ever more independent judicial systems faced with ever more similar problems, one nation's judges can and should learn from the experience of others. Those who oppose the use of foreign references distinguish historical practice, primarily on the ground that many of the foreign cases referenced came from nations with special jurisprudential ties to the United States, namely Britain or the British Commonwealth. They add that nothing prevents an American judge from learning about foreign case law by *reading* the work of others or corresponding with foreign colleagues. But, they say, an opinion's *supporting citation* wrongly smuggles a foreign view of a foreign law into a Constitution that is, and was meant to be, American in meaning and application. One distinguished judge wrote, "To cite foreign law as authority is to flirt with the discredited . . . idea of a universal natural law; or to suppose fantastically that the world's judges constitute a single elite community of wisdom and conscience."[7]

The second, far less controversial, problem arises out of the following circumstances: Many court cases involve foreign law; in such cases courts' references to foreign law are commonplace, often a necessity; and the number of those cases that find their way to American courts is growing rapidly. Indeed, in the year between *Lawrence* and *Roper* the Court considered or referred to foreign law in at least six "bread-and-butter" cases, cases that are important but do not involve such publicly controversial subject matter as *Lawrence's* homosexual rights or *Roper's* death penalty. The Court's use of foreign law in these six cases provoked no adverse comment. Everyone understood the need. The cases were unusual only in that their number, six out of a total docket of seventy-nine, indicates the increasingly routine nature of this kind of Court business.

Consider the subject matter of those cases: 1) Does American antitrust law authorize an Ecuadoran vitamin distributor to file suit in America against a Dutch vitamin producer? (The distributor says that the producer was a member of an unlawful vitamin price-fixing cartel operating *outside* the United States). 2) Does American "discovery" law permit one American firm to obtain documents from another American firm in order to present them to the European Union's anti-cartel Authority? (The Authority says it does not want them). 3) Does the American Foreign Sovereign Immunities Act bar Maria Altmann, an American citizen born in Austria, from bringing a federal court lawsuit in 2001 against the Austrian National Gallery to obtain possession of six Klimt paintings that she says the Nazis took from her uncle in 1938? 4) Does an environmental statute bar entry of trucks from Mexico—entry that the North American Free Trade Agreement authorizes the President to permit? 5) To what kinds of contemporary injuries today does the general language of the early-enacted (1789) American Alien Tort Statute apply? (The Statute permits compensation for injuries caused by actions "in violation of international law," and its authors likely intended the statute primarily to authorize compensation for injuries caused by pirates.) 6) Does the Warsaw Convention, governing international airline accidents, authorize recovery for a death caused by an allergy to cigarette smoke?[8]

In all these cases the parties expected the Court to look, and it did look, to international or foreign legal sources. In the antitrust and discovery cases, for example, several foreign nations (Germany, Japan, Canada, and France) and the European Union filed briefs. In the airline accident case all participating judges agreed that the Court must examine and treat as precedents Warsaw Convention cases decided in the courts of other nations. In applying the Alien Tort Statute, the Court had to determine today's equivalent of eighteenth-century piracy, and in doing so it consulted both older and modern international legal practice.

In Mrs. Altmann's case the decision of an intermediate Paris appeals court helped me better understand the "sovereign immunity" to which the American statute referred. Christian Dior had sued ex-King Farouk to collect a bill for dresses that the ex-King had bought for his wife before he lost his throne. The Paris court held that Farouk could no longer assert the sovereign immunity defense because he was no longer king. The decision thereby indicated that the Austrian National Gallery could no longer claim sovereign immunity, for (unlike the 1930s and 1940s) it was *now* engaged in commercial activities.

What problems does the growing number of these ordinary cases suggest? For one thing, American judges must better understand the requirements of foreign law. They must know where to look to find that law. They must be able to evaluate what they find. Many "foreign law" cases involve ordinary commercial activity. I once heard an eminent legal historian argue that contemporary British and American judges now enjoy institutional prestige that the eighteenth century British judiciary created through its development of workable commercial law, a development that helped Britain and America prosper. Today's comparable task is to assure the development of workable commercial law for an international economy.

That task, of course, belongs not simply to judges but to the bar and the law schools as well. Unless lawyers refer to foreign sources a judge is unlikely to discover what foreign law says or a foreign court has held. But unless lawyers have systematically learned how to locate foreign sources, they are unlikely to do so successfully. Law schools specialize in systematic training. And I suspect that lawyers will learn how and when to integrate foreign sources into an argument before a domestic court if the law schools integrate foreign source material into ordinary courses (say, commercial, procedural, or antitrust courses) rather than reserving all such matter for specialized courses in "international" or "comparative" law. Regardless, the need is there.

For another thing, the burgeoning "foreign law" caseload suggests a need to apply a purposive approach to textual interpretation. That is because a judge seeking to understand the meaning of a foreign statutory text cannot easily rely upon the literalist's interpretive tools—at least where the text is unclear and explanatory treatises fail to resolve the issue. In many foreign nations case law precedent has diminished legal force. And it makes little sense to rely upon, say, American "canons of interpretation," of which a foreign legislature was unaware.

It is often possible, however, for a judge to understand the basic purpose of a foreign text, consider consequences in light of that purpose, and apply the text accordingly. Thus, in Mrs. Altmann's case, the Paris court's determination helped an American judge interpret an American statute, not because a "canon of interpretation" led to the French conclusion or because the French court applied prior French precedent. Rather, that case helped because it explained the concept of sovereign immunity in terms of the basic purpose of that concept, namely the protection of current sovereigns from certain kinds of judicial interference. A consideration of consequences, here and abroad, also helped interpret the Alien Tort Statute. A broad interpretation would set a precedent for broad universal jurisdiction, and the latter would threaten differing and conflicting national court decisions, uncertainty, and unwarranted interference by one nation into the affairs of another. A narrow interpretation could avoid these risks. A purposive approach finds these and other consequences relevant, though not necessarily determinative. Similarly, the European nations' explanations of the detailed objectives of European antitrust enforcement mechanisms helped our Court understand the need to interpret American antitrust and discovery law so as to minimize the risk of unnecessary, counterproductive legal conflict.

Keeping in mind the value of a purposive approach, I return to the first problem—the problem of the use of foreign law in constitutional cases, for example, *Lawrence* and *Roper*. The subject matter of those two cases is special. Legal arguments about the death penalty and homosexual conduct can carry an emotional charge that may account for some of the attention the "foreign law" problem has received and some of the hostility to foreign references. Those who wish to limit interpretive tools to text, history, tradition, and precedent also oppose references to foreign law and practice—at least in so far as such references are not part of their more limited arsenal of interpretive weapons. But constitutional theory is not often the subject of intense Congressional debate. And I suspect that strong public hostility more likely reflects the public's concern that the judges are somehow smuggling foreign *values* into our American Constitution. Indeed, the fear I mentioned earlier, the fear that "judges" might think themselves "a single elite community of wisdom and conscience," reflects some such concern.

If the argument's heat reflects a concern about values, however, then an approach to constitutional interpretation that relies upon purpose and consequences may reduce the temperature. That is because purposive interpretation often treats the application of a constitutional provision as involving a practical problem. The examination of consequences (in light of the provision's underlying values) helps to resolve that problem. And learning what others have done can further that examination. From the purposive perspective the comparative activity will involve learning from foreign *experience,* not accepting foreign *values.*

Israel, for example, has had to reconcile a legal tradition protective of civil liberties with special demands flowing from terrorist threats. In doing so, it has found that military officials on the West Bank may, for reasons of military security, sometimes detain Israeli citizens without allowing them lawyers. But it has insisted that those officials justify to a neutral judicial official (in non-public proceedings) both the detention and the deprivation of counsel as necessary to meet strong security needs. And if the detention continues, the officials repeatedly must show a continued special need.

The British courts recently have considered and held invalid (under the European Convention on Human Rights) a British law that permits indefinitely long detention of terrorist suspects who were not British citizens. The government would appoint special counsel for the suspects. Counsel could challenge the government's evidentiary support in non-public proceedings. But they were not permitted to communicate with their clients.

The legal systems of Britain, Israel, and the United States differ in some respects, but they are similar in others. They are democracies. They have incorporated into their domestic law legal texts (embodied in Constitutions, charters, or statutes) that protect basic human rights. Their legal systems provide rights to counsel; they rarely authorize preventive detention, and they insist that judicial proceedings ordinarily take place in public. They recognized that sometimes special national security needs could modify normal civil liberties protection. Indeed, American Supreme Court Justices Jackson and Goldberg, recognizing the importance of balancing in the face of important national security interests, pointed out that the thirteen original States had not entered into a constitutional "suicide pact."

Given the legal similarities, there is little risk that an American judge who examined the foreign examples would adopt foreign values, i.e., values foreign to our own legal system. At the same time such an examination might help that judge learn about relevant consequences, about potential alternative ways of approaching a difficult practical problem, and about how other courts, foreign courts, have tried with greater or lesser success to reconcile similar conflicting values. That is to say, the foreign examples could help the American judge determine whether a particular kind of detention goes too far, whether it is unnecessarily restrictive, by indicating likely consequences and alternatives. Does American law require the government to justify repeatedly to a judicial official any continued need for special detention? What are the consequences of the British court's decision? Do similar problems exist, and are they significant, in the case at hand?

These kinds of questions are about practical needs, about difficulties and possibilities, not about values. And asking them may help judges, or other American officials, discover how better to reconcile security needs with traditional protection of basic human rights.

I do not claim that an examination of foreign law will always, or even often, provide a better answer to an American legal question. I do claim that it is a useful tool in the legal arsenal. And if Americans, who are pragmatists at heart, see that tool as even sometimes helpful to the resolution of a practical problem, they are likely to approve its use, even in highly visible, emotionally-charged legal cases, perhaps even in cases such as *Lawrence* and *Roper.*

In less visible cases, that approach, tied to text through underlying value, purpose, and consequence, may help to harmonize national laws. It might even further an interpretive "race to the top" encouraging judges to interpret texts as furthering those human purposes for which they were enacted.

Conclusion

I hope my examples suggest that the concept of active liberty can prove relevant in current discussion about European, as well as American, jurisprudence. The concept, after all, comes to America by way of Europe. It finds its origin in Greek political life. Benjamin Constant and others emphasized the need for modern governments to protect *both* ancient participative, and more modern individual, liberties. And today European law, like the American Constitution, seeks to assure democracies that also protect basic individual human liberty.

I also hope the examples reinforce the argument for a purposive approach to textual interpretation. That jurisprudential approach has a role to play outside, as well as inside, the United States. In particular, it can help reconcile laws of different nations, a matter of increasing importance as foreign laws increasingly affect the lives, not only of those who travel abroad, but also of those who live at home. If law can help achieve the human objectives of those whom it affects (and I optimistically believe it can), such an approach might bring about better law wherever we may seek it.

Notes

Chapter One: Active Liberty

1. Letter from Thomas Jefferson to William Charles Jarvis (Sept. 28, 1820), reprinted in 10 *The Writings of Thomas Jefferson 1816–1826*, at 160 (Paul Leicester Ford ed., 1899); Letter from Thomas Jefferson to Joseph C. Cabell (Feb. 2, 1816), reprinted in 1 *The Founders' Constitution*, at 142, 142 (Philip B. Kurland & Ralph Lerner eds., 1987); Letter from John Adams to Mercy Otis Warren (Apr. 16, 1776), *id.* at 670; e.g., The Federalist No. 28, at 178, 181 (Hamilton), (Clinton Rossiter ed., 1961) (discussing "invasions of the public liberty by national authority").

2. Benjamin Constant, *The Liberty of the Ancients Compared with That of the Moderns* (1819), in *Political Writings* 309, 309–28 (Biancamaria Fontana trans. & ed., 1988); Benjamin Constant, *De la liberté des Anciens: Discours prononcé à l'AthÉnÉe royal de Paris en 1819*, at 2, available at http://www.libres.org/francais/fondamentaux/liberte/liberte_constant.htm at 2; *Political Writings*, at 327; Constant, *De la liberté*; at 15.

3. Constant, *De la liberté*, at 2; *id.* at 7; *id.* at 13; in *Political Writings*, at 325–7.

4. Constant, *De la liberté*, at 14; in *Political Writings*, at 327.

5. See Constant, *De la liberté*; James B. Thayer, *John Marshall* 106 (1901); and Learned Hand, *The Spirit of Liberty* (3rd ed., 1960).

6. See Jack N. Rakove, *Original Meanings: Politics and Ideas in the Making of the Constitution* 11 (1996) (examining historical context surrounding framing and ratification of the

Constitution to understand constitutional interpretation);
Gordon Wood, *The Creation of the American Republic*
(1776–87) (1969); Bernard Bailyn, *The Ideological Origins of the
American Revolution* (1967); see also Akhil Reed Amar, *America's
Constitution: A Guided Tour* (2005).

7. Wood, *supra* note 6, at 574–80; see *id.* at 578 (quoting
   Adams ed., *Works of John Adams*, IV, 289, VI, 10, 89).

8. *Id.* at 164 (quoting "Boston's Instructions to its Representatives,"
   May 30, 1776, in Handlin, ed., *Popular Sciences*, 95).

9. *Id.* at 590.

10. *Id.* at 136; *id.* at 24–5 (quoting Boston Continental
    Journal, Jan. 15, 1778); *id* at 25 (quoting James Lovell, *An
    Oration Delivered April 2, 1771* [Boston, 1771] in Niles, ed.,
    Principles, 18).

11. Robert F. Williams, *The State Constitutions of the Founding
    Decade: Pennsylvania's Radical 1776 Constitution and Its
    Influences on American Constitutionalism*, 62 Temp. L. Rev. 541,
    547 (1989).

12. Wood, *supra* note 6, at 137; see *id.* at 412--13.

13. Alexander Meiklejohn, *Free Speech and Its Relation to
    Self-Government* 14–15 (1948).

14. U.S. Const. art. I; Wood, *supra* note 6, at 247 (quoting
    Benjamin Rush).

15. Edward S. Corwin, *The President, Office and Powers, 1787–1984*,
    at 45 (5th ed., 1984); see also *Congressional Quarterly Guide to
    the Presidency* 188 (Michael Nelson ed., 1996).

16. Wood, *supra* note 6, at 551 (quoting James Wilson).

17. *Id.* at 590.

18. The Federalist No. 10, at 77, 78 (Madison), (Clinton Rossiter
    ed., 1961); Wood, *supra* note 6, at 502; (quoting Madison, in
    Max Farrand, *Records of the Federal Convention of 1787*, I, at
    214 [1937]); Gordon S. Wood, *Representation in the American
    Revolution* 46 (1969) (quoting the Hartford Connecticut
    Courant, Nov. 27, 1786; Feb 5, 1787); Farrand, *Records of the
    Federal Convention of 1787*, I, at 562 (1937); *id.* at 253; Madison,
    The Federalist No. 10, at 80.

19. Wood, *supra* note 6, at 511; *id.* at 514 (quoting Madison in Farrand II at 204); *id.* (quoting letter from James Madison to Thomas Jefferson Oct. 24, 1787, Boyd, ed., *Jefferson Papers*, XII, 277–8); *id.* at 505 (quoting Federalist No. 10); Farrand, *supra* note 19, at 421.

20. See Akil Reed Amar, *The Supreme Court—1999 Term Foreward: The Document and the Doctrine*, 114 Harv. L. Rev. 26, 130–3 (2000).

21. Wood, *supra* note 6, at 164 (quoting Md. Decl. of Rts. [1770] V, Del. Decl. of Rts. [1776], *id.* at 408, 413.

22. *Id.* at 517.

23. Bailyn, *supra* note 6, at 55 (quoting James Madison).

24. The Federalist No. 39, at 240 (Madison).

25. The term "active liberty" is distinct from, but bears some similarities to, the philosopher Isaiah Berlin's concept of "positive liberty." See Isaiah Berlin, *Two Concepts of Liberty, Inaugural Lecture Before the University of Oxford* (Oct. 31, 1958), in *Four Essays on Liberty* 118, 118–72 (1969).

26. *Helvering v. Gregory*, 69 F.2d 809, 810–11 (1934) ("[T]he meaning of a sentence may be more than that of the separate words, as a melody is more than the notes"); see also Jerome Frank, *Words and Music: Some Remarks on Statutory Interpretation*, 47 Colum. L. Rev. 1259, 1262–4 (1947) (a "wise composer" expects performers to go beyond literal meaning in interpreting his score; a wise public should expect a judge to transcend technical meaning of the words in a statutory text).

27. U.S. Const. art. I; amends. XIV, XIX; *id.* art. IV.

28. See, e.g., *McCulloch v. Maryland*, 17 U.S. (4 Wheat.) 316 (1819) (upholding Congress's power to charter national bank); *Marbury v. Madison*, 5 U.S. (1 Cranch) 137 (1803) (establishing federal courts' power to review constitutionality of federal laws); see, e.g., *Giles v. Harris*, 189 U.S. 475 (1903) (refusing to enforce voting rights); *The Civil Rights Cases*, 109 U.S. 3 (1883) (narrowly interpreting Civil War amendments); *Lochner v. New York*, 198 U.S. 45 (1905)

(invalidating workplace health regulations on substantive due process grounds).

29. See, e.g., *Wickard v. Filburn*, 317 U.S. 111, 125 (1942) (rejecting distinction between "direct" and "indirect" effects on interstate commerce); *NLRB v. Jones & Laughlin Steel Corp.*, 301 U.S. 1 (1937) (upholding constitutionality of National Labor Relations Act and abandoning "indirect effects" test); *W. Coast Hotel Co. v. Parrish*, 300 U.S. 379 (1937) (concluding that minimum wage law for women did not violate constitutional right to freedom of contract); see, e.g., *Reynolds v. Sims*, 377 U.S. 533 (1964) (applying "one person, one vote" principle to state legislatures); *Baker v. Carr*, 369 U.S. 186 (1962) (finding that Equal Protection Clause justified federal court intervention to review voter apportionment); *Gomillion v. Lightfoot*, 364 U.S. 339 (1960) (striking down racial gerrymandering on Fifteenth Amendment grounds).

Chapter Two: Freedom of Speech

1. See, e.g., Alex Kozinski & Stuart Banner, *Who's Afraid of Commercial Speech?* 76 Va. L. Rev. 627, 631 (1990); Martin H. Redish, *The First Amendment in the Marketplace: Commercial Speech and the Values of Free Expression*, 39 Geo. Wash. L. Rev. 429, 448–52 (1971); cf. *44 Liquormart, Inc. v. Rhode Island*, 517 U.S. 484, 522 (1996) (Thomas, J., concurring in part and concurring in the judgment); U.S. Const. art. I.

2. Ctr. for Responsive Politics, *Election Overview, 2000 Cycle: Stats at a Glance*, at http://www.opensecrets.org/overview/index.asp? Cycle=2000 (accessed Mar. 8, 2002) (aggregating totals using Federal Election Commission data); Ctr. for Responsive Politics, *Election Overview*, at http://www.opensecrets.org/overview/stats.asp (accessed Nov. 21, 2003) (based on FEC data).

3. Alliance for Better Campaigns, *Dollars v. Discourse: Campaigns & Television*, at http://www.bettercampaigns.org/Doldisc/ camptv.htm (accessed Mar. 18, 2002); Lorraine

Woellert & Tom Lowry, *A Political Nightmare: Not Enough Airtime*, Business Week Online (Oct. 23, 2000), at http://www.businessweek.com/2000/00_43/b3704204.htm; see, e.g., G. W. Hogan, *Federal Republic of Germany, Ireland, and the United Kingdom: Three European Approaches to Political Campaign Regulation*, 21 Cap. U. L. Rev. 501, 523 (1992).

4. Taken from the record developed in *McConnell v. Federal Election Comm'n*, No. 02–1674 et al., Joint Appendix 1558.

   In the 2002 midterm election, less than one-tenth of one per cent of the population gave 83 per cent of all (hard and soft) itemized campaign contributions. Ctr. for Responsive Politics, see *supra* note 2.

5. Taken from the record developed in *McConnell*, No. 02–1674 et al., Joint Appendix 1564.

6. *Buckley v. Valeo*, 424 U.S. 1 (1976); *McConnell v. FEC*, 540 U.S. 93 (2003).

7. The Federalist No. 57, at 351 (Madison).

8. U.S. Const. amend. I.

9. *Masses Publishing Co. v. Patten*, 244 F. 535, 540 (S.D.N.Y. 1917 [(Hand, J.)]); Benjamin Constant, *The Liberty of the Ancients Compared with That of the Moderns* (1819), in *Political Writings*, at 327 (Biancamaria Fontana trans. & ed., 1988).

10. *McConnell*, 540 U.S. at 136, 231; see also *Nixon v. Shrink Mo. Gov't PAC*, 528 U.S. 377, 399–402 (2000) (Breyer, J., concurring); *id.* at 136 (internal quotation marks omitted); *id.* at 137 (internal quotation marks omitted); see *Board of Trade of Chicago v. United States*, 246 U.S. 231 (1918); see *McConnell*, 540 U.S. at 134–42.

11. *McConnell*, 540 U.S. at 137.

12. *Nike v. Kasky*, 539 U.S. 654 (2003).

13. *Thompson v. Western States Medical Center*, 535 U.S. 357 (2002).

14. *Nike*, 539 U.S. at 665 (Breyer, J., dissenting from the order dismissing the writ of certiorari as improvidently granted); *Thompson*, 535 U.S. at 378 (Breyer, J., dissenting).
15. See *Nike*, 539 U.S. at 656–8 (Stevens, J., concurring); *id.* at 665 (Breyer, J., dissenting).
16. *Thompson*, 535 U.S. 361–4.
17. *Id.* at 374; *id.* at 384 (Breyer, J., dissenting) (quoting Rosenthal, Berndt, Donohue, Frank, & Epstein, *Promotion of Prescription Drugs to Consumers*, 346 New Eng. J. Med. 498–505 [2002], citing Lipsky, *The Opinions and Experiences of Family Physicians Regarding Direct-to-Consumer Advertising*, 45 J. Fam. Pract. 495–9 [1997]), *id.* at 379.

Chapter Three: Federalism

1. See, e.g., *Gregory v. Ashcroft*, 501 U.S. 452, 458 (1991) ("This federalist structure of joint sovereigns preserves to the people numerous advantages. It assures a decentralized government that will be more sensitive to the diverse needs of a heterogeneous society; it increases opportunity for citizen involvement in democratic processes; it allows for more innovation and experimentation in government; and it makes government more responsive by putting the States in competition for a mobile citizenry."); *New State Ice Co. v. Liebmann*, 285 U.S. 262, 311 (1932) (Brandeis, J., dissenting).
2. *New York v. United States*, 505 U.S. 144 (1992); *Printz v. United States*, 521 U.S. 898 (1997).
3. *Printz*, 521 U.S. at 940 (Stevens, J., dissenting).
4. See, e.g., *Fed. Mar. Comm'n v. S.C. State Ports Auth.*, 535 U.S. 743, 749–50 (2002) ("Congress, pursuant to its Article I powers, cannot abrogate state sovereign immunity..."); *Bd. of Trustees v. Garrett*, 531 U.S. 356, 364 (2001) (same); *Kimel v. Fla. Bd. of Regents*, 528 U.S. 62, 78 (2000) (same); *Fla. Prepaid Postsecondary Educ. Expense Bd. v. Coll. Sav. Bank*, 527 U.S. 627, 636, 144 (Congress cannot abrogate state sovereign immunity pursuant to the Patent Clause of Article I); *Seminole Tribe of Fla. v. Fla.*, 517 U.S. 44, 72 (1996)

(Fourteenth Amendment is the only recognized source of authority for abrogation).

5. See *Fed. Mar. Comm'n* 535 U.S. at 748–51 (2002).
6. *United States v. Lopez*, 514 U.S. 549 (1995) (striking down Gun-Free School Zones Act as an invalid exercise of Congress's commerce power); *United States v. Morrison*, 529 U.S. 598 (2000) (holding unconstitutional certain provisions of the Violence Against Women Act as an invalid exercise of the commerce power).
7. *Morrison*, 529 U.S. at 658 (Breyer, J., dissenting); *id.* at 617–18 ("We accordingly reject the argument that Congress may regulate noneconomic, violent criminal conduct based solely on that conduct's aggregate effect on interstate commerce. The Constitution requires a distinction between what is truly national and what is truly local").
8. See, e.g., *Nev. Dep't of Human Res. v. Hibbs*, 538 U.S. 721 (2003); *Frew v. Hawkins*, 540 U.S. 431 (2003).
9. Laurence H. Tribe, *American Constitutional Law* §§6–1 to –2 (3d ed. 2000); *C & A Carbone, Inc. v. Clarkstown*, 511 U.S. 383, 401–02 (O'Connor, J., concurring); see, e.g., *Camps Newfound/Owatonna v. Town of Harrison*, 520 U.S. 564 (1997); *Pike v. Bruce Church*, 397 U.S. 137, 145 (1970); also, *Wyoming v. Oklahoma*, 502 U.S. 437 (1992) (striking down Oklahoma law that discriminated against out-of-state coal).
10. See, e.g., *Quill Corp. v. North Dakota ex rel. Heitkamp*, 504 U.S. 298, 318 (1992); *Lewis v. BT Inv. Managers, Inc.*, 447 U.S. 27, 44 (1980).
11. See, e.g., Guido Calabresi, *The Supreme Court, 1990 Term—Foreword: Antidiscrimination and Constitutional Accountability (What the Bork-Brennan Debate Ignores)*, 105 Harv. L. Rev. 80, 103–08 (1991); cf. Alexander M. Bickel & Harry H. Wellington, *Legislative Purpose and the Judicial Process*, 71 Harv. L. Rev. 1 (1957); Guido Calabresi, *Common Law for the Age of Statutes* 120–4 (1982); also, *Gregory v. Ashcroft*, 501 U.S. 452 (1991) (requiring "clear statement" by

Congress when it legislates in an area traditionally regulated by states); Larry J. Obhof, *Federalism, I Presume? A Look at the Enforcement of Federalism Principles Through Presumptions and Clear Statement Rules,* 2004 Mich. St. L. Rev. 123.

Chapter Four: The Right of Privacy

1. Jeffrey Rosen, *The Unwanted Gaze: The Destruction of Privacy in America* (2000). Thinkers who embrace this concept of privacy stand on the shoulders of Justice Brandeis, who first articulated the right to privacy in these terms—the "right to be let alone"—in his dissent in *Olmstead v. United States,* 277 U.S. 438, 478 (1928) (Brandeis, J., dissenting). See also Samuel D. Warren & Louis D. Brandeis, *The Right to Privacy,* 4 Harv. L. Rev. 193 (1890); see, e.g., Charles Fried, *Privacy,* 77 Yale L. J. 475, 477–8, 484–6 (1968); Ruth Gavison, *Privacy and the Limits of Law,* 89 Yale L. J. 421, 455 (1980) ("Privacy is . . . essential to democratic government because it fosters and encourages the moral autonomy of the citizen, a central requirement of a democracy"); Lawrence Lessig, *Code and Other Laws of Cyberspace* 153–55 (1999).
2. E.g., 18 U.S.C. § 2511 (1994 & Supp. II 1997) (regulating electronic surveillance), and 15 U.S.C. § 6802 (Supp. V 2000) (regulating disclosure of personal information by financial institutions).
3. Alexis de Tocqueville, *Democracy in America* 232 (Harvey C. Mansfield and Delba Winthrop trans., University of Chicago, 2000) (1835).
4. *Bartnicki v. Vopper,* 532 U.S. 514, 518–19 (2001); 18 U.S.C. § 2511(1) (c) (1994); see also *Bartnicki, supra,* at 523–4.
5. *Bartnicki,* 532 U.S. at 532–5; *id.* at 535–41 (Breyer, J., concurring), at 540–1.
6. *Kyllo v. United States,* 533 U.S. 27, 40 (2001); *id.* at 33–4.

Chapter Five: Affirmative Action

1. *Grutter v. Bollinger,* 539 U.S. 306 (2003); *id.* at 313–14, 315–16.
2. *Id.* at 318, 315, 316.

3. U.S. Const. amend. XIV, section 1.
4. *Grutter*, 539 U.S. at 353–4 (Thomas, J., dissenting) (quoting *Adarand Constructors, Inc. v. Pena*, 515 U.S. 200, 240 [1995] [Thomas, J., concurring in part and concurring in judgement]).
5. *Grutter*, 539 U.S. 244, 298 (2003) (Ginsburg, J., dissenting).
6. *Adarand*, 515 U.S. at 275 (Ginsburg, J., dissenting); *id*. at 276.
7. *Grutter*, 539 U.S. at 326, 328, 334, 343.
8. *United States v. Jefferson County Bd. of Educ.*, 372 F.2d 834, 876 (5th Cir. 1966); *Grutter*, 539 U.S. at 316; *Wygant v. Jackson Bd. of Ed.*, 476 U.S. 267, 278 & n. 5 (1986); see also *Richmond v. J. A. Croson Co.*, 488 U.S. 469, 496–8 (1988).
9. *Regents of the University of California v. Bakke*, 438 U.S. 265, 312 (1978) (opinion of Powell, J.); *Grutter*, 539 U.S. at 330 (internal citations and quotation marks omitted); *id*. at 330.
10. *Grutter*, 539 U.S. at 330.
11. *Id*. at 331.
12. *Id*. at 330–1 (internal citations and quotation marks omitted).
13. *Id*. at 331, 332 (internal citations and quotation marks omitted) (emphasis added).
14. Cf. John Hart Ely, *Democracy and Distrust* 135–79 (1980) (discussing representation-reinforcing theory of judicial review and constitutional interpretation).

Chapter Six: Statutory Interpretation

1. Aharon Barak, *A Judge on Judging: The Role of a Supreme Court in a Democracy*, 116 Harv. L. Rev. 28–9 (2002).
2. See, e.g., Antonin Scalia, *Common-Law Courts in a Civil-Law System: The Role of United States Federal Courts in Interpreting the Constitution and Laws*, in *A Matter of Interpretation: Federal Courts and the Law* 26–7 (Amy Gutmann ed., 1997); see William N. Eskridge Jr., Philip P. Frickey, & Elizabeth Garrett, *Cases and Materials on Legislation—Statutes and the Creation of Public Policy* 822 (3d ed., 2001); Frank H. Easterbrook, *Text, History, and*

Structure in Statutory Interpretation, 17 Harv. J. L. & Pub. Pol'y 61, 64 (1994).

3. 28 U.S.C. § 1602 *et seq*; 28 U.S.C. §§ 1441(d), 1602; 28 U.S.C. § 1603(b)(2).
4. See *Dole Food Co. v. Patrickson*, 538 U.S. 468 (2003).
5. *Id.* at 476; *id.* at 477 (quoting *United States v. Nordic Village, Inc.*, 503 U.S. 30, 36 [1992]).
6. *Id.* at 485 (Breyer, J., concurring in part and dissenting in part); *id.* at 485–6; *Flink v. Paladini*, 279 U.S. 59, 63 (1929).
7. 9 U.S.C. § 1 *et seq; id.* § 1 (emphasis added); *Circuit City Stores v. Adams*, 532 U.S. 105 (2001); *id.* at 114; id. at 114–15 (quoting 2A N. Singer, *Sutherland on Statutes and Statutory Construction* § 47.17 [1991]).
8. *Circuit City Stores*, 532 U.S. 105 at 115–16; *id.* at 117.
9. *Id.* at 124 (Stevens, J., dissenting), 126–7 (Stevens, J., dissenting), 127 (Stevens, J., dissenting), (citations omitted).
10. *Id.* at 135–37 (Souter, J., dissenting).
11. 28 U.S.C. § 2244(d)(1) (Supp. II 1997); *id.* § 2244(d)(2) (emphasis added); *Duncan v. Walker*, 533 U.S. 167 (2001).
12. *Duncan*, 533 U.S. 167 at 185 (Breyer, J., dissenting) (citing U.S. Dept. of Justice, Office of Justice Programs, Bureau of Justice Statistics, *Federal Habeas Corpus Review: Challenging State Court Criminal Convictions* 17 ([1995]).
13. See *id.* at 172–5.
14. *Id.* at 190–3 (Breyer, J., dissenting)
15. *Id.* at 190 (Breyer, J., dissenting).
16. Barak, *supra* note 1, at 28–9.

Chapter Seven: Administrative Law

1. *Chevron USA v. Natural Resources Defense Council, Inc.*, 467 U.S. 837 (1984); *id.* at 843 (quoting *Morton v. Ruiz*, 415 U.S. 199, 231 [1974]); *id.* at 844; *Christensen v. Harris County*, 529 U.S. 576, 589 fn. (Scalia, J., concurring).
2. 5 U.S.C. § 7114(a)(4); *Nat'l Fed'n of Fed. Emples., Local 1309 v. DOI*, 526 U.S. 86, 88 (1999).

3. See *Packard Motor Car Co. v. NLRB*, 330 U.S. 485 (1947); see *Gen. Dynamics Land Sys. v. Cline*, 540 U.S. 581 (2004).
4. Cf. *United States v. Mead Corp.*, 533 U.S. 218, 221 (2001).

Chapter Eight: Purposive Interpretation

1. *The Supreme Court Compendium* 210 (Lee Epstein et al. eds. 2003) (showing annual data for, *inter alia*, the years 1994–2001); *id.* at 225.
2. *The Words of Justice Brandeis* 61 (Solomon Goldman ed., 1953); *Int'l News Service v. AP*, 248 U.S. 215, 267 (1918) (Brandeis, J., dissenting); *Lochner v. New York*, 198 U.S. 45, 75 (1905) (Holmes, J., dissenting); Learned Hand, *The Spirit of Liberty* 109 (3d ed., 1960); *Otis v. Parker*, 187 U.S. 606, 609 (1903) (Holmes, J.).
3. Hand, *supra* note 2, at 109; *United States v. Classic*, 313 U.S. 299, 316 (1941) (Stone, J.); Hand, *supra* at 157; Aharon Barak, *A Judge on Judging: The Role of a Supreme Court in a Democracy*, 116 Harv. L. Rev. 16, 28 (2002) ("The law regulates relationships between people. It prescribes patterns of behavior. It reflects the values of society. The role of the judge is to understand the purpose of law in society and to help the law achieve its purpose."); Goldman, *supra* note 2, at 115; Felix Frankfurter, *Some Reflections on the Reading of Statutes*, 47 Colum. L. Rev. 527, 541 (1947).
4. Felix Frankfurter, *The Supreme Court in the Mirror of Justices*, in *Of Law and Life & Other Things That Matter* 94 (Philip B. Kurland ed., 1965); *id.* at 95; Hand, *supra* note 2, at 109; *New State Ice Co. v. Liebmann*, 285 U.S. 262, 311 (1932) (Brandeis, J., dissenting); Frankfurter, *supra* at 95.
5. Frankfurter, *supra* note 4, at 95; *Otis v. Parker*, 187 U.S. at 609 (Holmes, J.); cf. Hand, *supra* note 2, at 162 (referring to "every conceivable allowance for differences of outlook"); *id.* at 190.
6. Thurgood Marshall, *Reflections on the Bicentennial of the United States Constitution*, 101 Harv. L. Rev. 1, 2 (1987) ("When the Founding Fathers used" the phrase "We the People," they "did not have in mind the majority of America's citizens").

Compare Herbert Wechsler, *Toward Neutral Principles of Constitutional Law*, 33 Harv. L. Rev. 1 (1959) (suggesting that *Brown v. Board of Education* had no sound grounding), with Louis Pollak, Race, Law, & History: The Supreme Court from "Dred Scott" to "*Grutter v. Bollinger*," Daedalus, Winter 2005, at 29, 40–1 (indicating that Wechsler changed his mind and found clarity in the principle that "an invidious assessment may no longer be prescribed by law or by official action," but that race can be taken into account to "correct inequalities of opportunity that may be found").

7. See, e.g., Antonin Scalia, *A Matter of Interpretation: Federal Courts and the Law* (1997).

8. Jack N. Rakove, *Original Meanings: Politics and Ideas in the Making of the Constitution* 339–65 (1996).

9. U.S. Const. amend. IX; Bernard Bailyn, *The Living Past—Commitments for the Future*, Remarks at the First Millennium Evening at the White House (Feb. 11, 1998), http://clinton4.nara.gov/Initiatives/Millennium/bbailyn.html.

10. See *Plessy*, 163 U.S. 537 (1896); see *Brown*, 347 U.S. 483 (1954).

11. See Stephen Breyer, *Judicial Review: A Practicing Judge's Perspective*, 78 Tex. L. Rev. 761, 769 (2000) (referring to Justice O'Connor's analogy).

12. U.S. Const. amend. I; *Zelman v. Simmons-Harris*, 536 U.S. 639, 717 (2000) (Breyer, J., dissenting); *id.* at 718; *id.* at 719–21; *id.* at 718–23 (citing, *inter alia, Lee v. Weisman*, 505 U.S. 577 [1992], and *Committee for Public Ed. & Religious Liberty v. Nyquist*, 413 U.S. 756, 794 [1973]).

13. *Committee for Public Ed.*, 413 U.S. 756.

14. *Van Orden v. Perry*, No. 03–1500 (June 27, 2004) (Breyer, J., concurring in the judgment), *slip op.*, at 1.

15. See Karl N. Llewellyn, *The Common Law Tradition: Deciding Appeals* 525 (1960); William N. Eskridge Jr. and Phillip P. Frickey, *Cases and Materials on Legislation: Statutes and the Creation of Public Policy* 652–3 (2d ed. 1995) (noting tension between these canons).

16. *Stogner v. California*, 539 U.S. 607 (2003); *Calder v. Bull*, 3 Dall. 386, 390 (1798); cf. 2 R. Wooddeson, *A Systematical View of the Laws of England* 638–9 (1792).
17. *Stogner*, 539 U.S. at 622–6, 642–9 (Kennedy, J., dissenting), 622–6, 642–9.
18. 15 U.S.C. § 14 (2004); see *Northern Pacific RR Co. v. United States*, 356 U.S. 1, 5–6 (1958) (A tying arrangement is "an agreement by a party to sell one product but only on the condition that the buyer also purchases a different [or tied] product, or at least agrees that he will not purchase that product from any other supplier").
19. *Lockyer v. Andrade*, 538 U.S. 63 (2003); *Ewing v. California*, 538 U.S. 11 (2003); *Ewing*, 538 U.S. at 31–32 (Scalia, J., concurring in the judgment); *id.* at 32 (Thomas, J., concurring in the judgement).
20. *Id.* at 35, 52–53 (Breyer, J., dissenting).
21. Declaration of Independence (emphasis added).
22. See, e.g., Nat'l Ctr. for Educ. Statistics, U.S. Dep't. of Educ., *The NAEP 1998 Civics Report Card* (1999); Nat'l Constitution Center Survey (1998), at http://www.constitutioncenter.org/CitizenAction/CivicResearchResults/NCCTeens'Poll.shtml; Lydia Saad, *Americans' Faith in Government Shaken but Not Shattered by Watergate*, at http://www.galluppoll.com (June 19, 1997) (subscriber content).
23. See, e.g., Council for Excellence in Government, *A Matter of Trust: Americans and Their Government: 1958–2004*, at 4–5 (2004); Center for Information and Research in Civic Learning & Engagement, *Short Term Impacts, Long Term Opportunities*, 4 (2002); Alexis de Tocqueville, *Democracy in America*, 234–35 (Harvey C. Mansfield and Delba Winthrop trans., University of Chicago 2000) (1835).
24. See Saad, *supra* note 22 (explaining that, in 1997, public trust in Judicial Branch exceeded trust in Executive and Legislative Branches).
25. Thucydides, *The Peloponnesian War* 108–15 (Thomas Hobbes trans., Univ. of Chi. Press 1989) (1629) (quoting "The Funeral

Notes to pages 132–158

Oration of Pericles"); letter from John Adams to Mercy
Otis Warren (Apr. 16, 1776) reprinted in 1 *The Founder's
Constitution,* 670 (Philip B. Kurland and Ralph Lerner
eds., 1987).

Chapter Nine: A Broader Application

1. *Leyla Şahin v. Turkey,* no. 44774/98 (2005), European Court of
   Human Rights (Strasbourg)
2. *Leyla Şahin v. Turkey,* § 113–115.
3. *Leyla Şahin v. Turkey,* § 55–65.
4. *Karduman v. Turkey,* no. 16278/90, Commission decision of 3
   May 1993; *Dahlab v. Switzerland,* no. 42393/98, ECHR 2001-V.
5. See http://eur-lex.europa.eu/en/treaties/index.htm
6. *Lawrence v Texas,* 539 U.S. 558 (2003); *Roper v Simmons,* 543 U.S.
   551 (2005).
7. Judge Richard Posner, *Legal Affairs,* July/August 2004, at
   www.legalaffairs.org
8. 1) *F. Hoffmann-La Roche Ltd et. al. v. Empagran S.A. et al* 124 S. Ct.
   2359, 2369 (2004); 2) *Intel Corporation v. Advanced Micro Devices,
   Inc.* 542 U.S. 241 (2004); 3) *Republic of Austria v. Altmann,* 126
   S. Ct. 1210 (2004); 4) *Department of Transportation v. Publiccitizen*
   541 U.S. 752 (2004) ; 5) *Sosa v. Alvarez-Machain et al.* 542 U.S. 692
   (2004); 6) *Olympic Airways v. Husain* 540 U.S. 644 (2004).

Index

Index

Index

Index

speech *see* **freedom of speech**
freedom of religion
  active liberty 137, 141 *see also*
    active liberty
  empirical factors 138–41
  fundamentalist movements
    135, 138
  human rights
  religious belief 132
  religious teaching 132
  Islamic dress 131, 133, 134,
    138–41
  judicial impartiality 141
  judicial precedent 136
  margin of appreciation 133,
    134, 136, 137, 139, 140
  religious diversity *see*
    religious diversity
  restrictions
    justified 132, 134, 140, 141
    legal restrictions 137
    necessary 133, 137, 138
    protection of other rights
      133, 137
    public health 133
    public morals 133
    public order 133
    public safety 133
  secularism 133, 134, 135, 138
freedom of speech
  active liberty 37, 38 *see also*
    active liberty
  constitutional protection
    34, 35
  disclosure of information 35
  elected officials 37

free expression 34, 63, 77
government regulation
  business practices 45, 46
  campaign finance 34, 36,
    38, 41, 50
  communication law 36
  consumer protection 35
  corporate advertising 34,
    35, 45, 46
  disclosure of information
    35
  discrimination law 35
  economic regulation 34, 37
  false advertising 48
  health law 35
  judicial review 37, 38, 40–7
  limits 36, 49
  network access 36
  pharmaceutical
    information 34, 46, 47,
    48, 125
  product labelling 35
  product safety 50
  proportionality 44
  securities law 35
  tobacco advertising 35
  unconstitutional 34
  warranty law 35
information society 35
lawful restriction 43
political process 37
presumption of
  unconstitutionality
  commercial speech 34, 37,
    45, 49
  mid-range presumption 34

Index

Index